THE HANDBOOK FOR
EFFECTIVE EMERGENCY AND
CRISIS MANAGEMENT

THE HANDBOOK FOR EFFECTIVE EMERGENCY AND CRISIS MANAGEMENT

Mayer Nudell

Norman Antokol

Lexington Books

D.C. Heath and Company/Lexington, Massachusetts/Toronto

This book is published as part of the Lexington Books *Issues in Low-Intensity Conflict* series, Neil C. Livingstone, consulting editor.

Library of Congress Cataloging-in-Publication Data

Nudell, Mayer.
  The handbook for effective emergency and crisis
management.

  (Lexington Books issues in low-intensity conflict
series)
  Bibliography: p.
  Includes index.
  1. Crisis management—United States.   I. Antokol,
Norman.   II. Title.   III. Series.
HD49.N83   1988   658.4   87–45997
ISBN 0–669–17140–9 (alk. paper)

Published simultaneously in Canada
Printed in the United States of America
International Standard Book Number: 0–669–17140–9
Library of Congress Catalog Card Number: 87–45997

The paper used in this publication meets the minimum requirements of
American National Standard for Information Sciences—Permanence of
Paper for Printed Library Materials, ANSI Z39.48-1984.

∞™

ISBN 0–669–17140–9

88 89 90 91 92 8 7 6 5 4 3 2 1

CONTENTS

To the memory of Faye Falk Antokol and to Ben and Leah Nudell.

We also dedicate this book to the unsung heroes of emergency response—the men and women who fight the daily battles to ensure that their organizations are prepared in case of emergency.

FIGURES AND TABLES

TABLES

FOREWORD

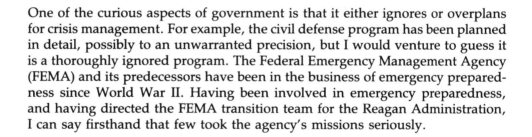

One of the curious aspects of government is that it either ignores or overplans for crisis management. For example, the civil defense program has been planned in detail, possibly to an unwarranted precision, but I would venture to guess it is a thoroughly ignored program. The Federal Emergency Management Agency (FEMA) and its predecessors have been in the business of emergency preparedness since World War II. Having been involved in emergency preparedness, and having directed the FEMA transition team for the Reagan Administration, I can say firsthand that few took the agency's missions seriously.

A case in point occurred in 1971 when President Richard Nixon implemented the "Wage-Price-Rent-Freeze." Direct economic controls were imposed. The Office of Emergency Preparedness (OEP)—a White House agency—was in charge of implementing the president's wishes. Since the birth of OEP and its forerunners, a great deal of attention has been paid to economic stabilization. In fact, OEP had an "economic stabilization division."

When the freeze was announced the division went into action, fulfilling its one real mission. Oddly enough, nobody paid attention to it. So, there we were! In a sense we were in charge of running the nation for ninety days, but all our planning was thrown out and we were left to our own devices.

One can point to a variety of examples, including large-scale natural disasters. Hurricane Agnes caused widespread destruction. Allocating state and national assets to meet the needs of the many hurricane victims proved excruciating. Eventually, after a lot of politics and human suffering, the crisis abated. There was, of course, a large political price to pay. As one would have expected, the cause of crisis management was dealt a severe blow.

Though it may be somewhat cynical, one cannot help but observe that emergency managers plan to cope with either little or massive disasters. The little ones go away on their own and the really big ones are acts of God. The emergency manager also must contend with difficult in-between cases, such as a large chemical spill or a terrorist attack upon natural gas transmission.

While there are a relatively small number of true believers in emergency planning, there are an extraordinary number of would-be swashbucklers who are willing to jump in, having never made the slightest preparations. This was particularly true of the U.S. counterterrorism program during the Ford and Carter years.

A fundamental point is that crises do occur and they are not fully predictable. Government and industry would be better off with thoughtful crisis managers. We must spend the time to study likely disasters and develop a rich set of scenarios, simulate operational problems of a major event, and determine who are the most knowledgeable about the operations of government or large companies.

These tasks are not easy. Most important, really good people are difficult to find. Most large organizations, whether in government or industry, rarely think beyond the first move. Large companies do plan, but few top executives pay serious attention to the crisis management function or its products. Until recently, government had not undertaken the planning necessary to cope with large-scale crises. Industry is just beginning.

Government and industry face many hazards: natural disasters, environmental incidents, and terrorism are but a few. Emergency management strategies can be devised rationally and protocols can be tailored individually to meet the needs of government agencies, companies, and the public. All face command, control, and communications problems as well as risk assessment. Large organizations, governmental and private, are at risk if they do not consider prophylactic measures and simulate operational problems. No one can predict the future confidently, but considerable advance planning can be done. Mayer Nudell and Norman Antokol have given form to an otherwise amorphous subject, translating abstract issues into practical exercises and procedures. The book is really worthwhile reading. Over time, a lot will be said about the subject. The Nudell-Antokol book will be referenced widely.

—*Robert H. Kupperman*

AUTHORS' NOTE

We remind readers that crisis management and emergency response are inexact sciences that are constantly evolving. The suggestions and recommendations we make in this book are the result of our experience and our understanding of the experiences of others. While we believe that they constitute a firm foundation for use in emergencies, they are neither a panacea nor a guarantee of success. Each crisis has its own dynamic and our suggestions may need to be modified or augmented accordingly. Common sense and a good grasp of your particular circumstances should always be your guide.

ACKNOWLEDGMENTS

It is impossible to produce a work such as this without the invaluable assistance of a number of people. The authors especially would like to note that the following people provided us with considerable information and help: Renee Bafalis, Office of Foreign Disaster Assistance; Steve Skolochenko, U.S. Postal Service; Eugene Mastrangelo, Risks International Division, Business Risks International; Joseph Reap, Office of Counterterrorism, Department of State. Our thanks also to Colonel (Ret.) Murl Munger of the Army War College, Leah Nudell, and Peter Fenn for their efforts on our behalf. We owe especial gratitude to the editors and production staff of Lexington Books whose support and help made this a better book. There were others who also provided us with invaluable assistance, but they prefer to remain anonymous. Our thanks to them all— particularly to Marilyn, Barbara, and Maria Elena who suffered more than the slings and arrows of outrageous fortune while we put it all together.

We accept entire responsibility for the conclusions we have drawn and for any errors or omissions in our data.

UNDERSTANDING CRISES

1

Shortly after 4:00 A.M. on the morning of March 28, 1979, a series of pumps supplying water to steam generators malfunctioned at Three Mile Island, in Pennsylvania. Steam is critical in the operation of a nuclear reactor, not only for the production of electricity, but also to carry off some of the intense heat carried by the reactor water. With no water flowing in, there could be no steam, so the safety system automatically shut down the steam turbine and the electric generator to which it was connected. The temperature of the reactor coolant began to rise and pressure started to build.

A relief valve opened automatically, and steam and water started to drain away, but the pressure continued to rise. So, the reactor shut itself down; its control rods dropped into its core, automatically stopping the fission process and the heat that would otherwise have continued to be generated.

However, decaying radioactive material left from the fission process could still cause the reactor's coolant water to overheat. Three emergency pumps that had begun operating when the main pumps malfunctioned now began carrying off *the coolant water, keeping the reactor's core from overheating. The safety system was working perfectly, and as soon as the relief valve closed automatically, the incident would be over.*

But the valve didn't close, and the operators on duty in the control room failed to realize it was stuck open. In the next couple of hours, more than one-third of the reactor's entire coolant capacity would be lost, and the danger of a nuclear meltdown would become a stark reality. The result, had the worst actually come to pass, could have been the destruction of a huge area and the deaths of millions of people.

The worst didn't happen, but the results for General Public Utilities Corporation were bad enough. Cleanup and repairs at Three Mile Island have taken up most of the 1980s and cost close to a billion dollars. The company has been the target of hundreds of lawsuits—some of which have led to settlements in the hundreds of thousands, even millions, of dollars. Eleven criminal indictments were handed down by a federal grand jury, to most of which the utility pleaded nolo contendere, *or no contest. And the setback to public confidence in nuclear energy in the United States—which was originally to have been the cornerstone of our energy policy in the twenty-first century—is incalculable.*

Are you and your organization ready for the next crisis? Have you formulated your plans? Are they current? Do your people know their responsibilities and authority during an emergency? Will your procedures work? These are just a few of the questions you must know the answers to if you and your organization are to successfully deal with your next crisis.

A crisis represents both dangers and opportunities. If your response to it is merely reactive, the dangers will outweigh the opportunities. The damage to you and your organization will be magnified by a public perception of failure, regardless of how good your response was. Even the most successful organization can be stigmatized unfairly for years to come.

On the other hand, effective crisis management can not only limit the actual damage sustained by your organization, it also permits you to affect the public's perception of the crisis and your organization's response. Effective crisis management can also pay dividends in terms of intraorganizational relations.

Increasingly, there are substantial financial, legal, personnel, and other penalties attached to unpreparedness in the face of an emergency—especially when it can be established that a prudent person could have foreseen the possibility of the emergency. **A crisis is not the time for ad hoc responses.** Planning for *all* foreseeable contingencies is a form of insurance that should not be rejected. The relatively small commitment of time, personnel, and resources is insignificant in the face of the possible damage from even the smallest disaster or induced catastrophe.

A classic example of the value of a contingency plan—and the dangers of not having one—was furnished by Procter and Gamble in the matter of Rely Tampons. Evidence existed to suggest a link between the tampons and Toxic Shock Syndrome months before the U.S. Food and Drug Administration formally contacted the parent company. Because the evidence wasn't conclusive, however, the makers adopted a wait-and-see attitude. If they had formed a plan about what to do *in case* a link was proved, they would have saved themselves a lot of trouble. We emphasize the point again—crisis management is not just anticipating what is likely to happen; it is thinking the unthinkable *before* it happens.

When considering crisis planning and preparations, it is important to remember that a crisis can stem from any number of emergencies. This said, however, all emergencies fall within two broad categories: disasters and induced catastrophes. Understanding the difference is important.

DISASTERS

A disaster is an overwhelming ecological disruption occurring on a scale sufficient to require outside assistance.[1] It differs from other types of emergencies in that it is a natural occurrence or the result of an accident. It is not the result of any intentional action taken by any human agency. This category of emergency would include floods, earthquakes, famines, hurricanes, disease, volcanic eruption, crashes, industrial accidents, fires, landslides, avalanches, and so forth. Between 1900 and April 1987, 2,553 major disasters occurred outside the United States.[2] India, the most affected foreign country with 192 disasters during this period, had fourteen disasters in 1986 alone.[3] Interestingly, in any given year, there are more disasters within the United States than in any other country.[4] For example, between 1947 and 1981, one-third of all disasters worldwide occurred in the United States, according to one authority.[5] Fortunately for Americans, although the dollar value of damage from disasters tends to be high, deaths tend to be low.[6] This is not the case in other countries.

INDUCED CATASTROPHES

This is the category of emergency commonly associated with crisis management in the public mind. It includes arson, bombings, kidnappings, hostage/barricade situations, hijackings, extortion, product tampering/contamination, and other acts of terrorism. (It also includes financial, corporate management, and most general business emergencies, although these nonsecurity situations require responses that are outside the scope of this book.) These are emergencies that directly result from intentional actions taken by individuals or groups. Occasionally these induced catastrophes result when events get out of the control of those who begin them (for example, when a protest march becomes a riot), but they are always the result of conscious decisions.

THE COMMONALITIES

Regardless of the type of crisis with which you are dealing, there are a number of common requirements if you are to be successful. These generic requirements form the basis for this book. They include:

- deciding policy

- assessing threat

- identifying resources

- selecting crisis team personnel

- locating the crisis management center

- equipping the crisis center

- training crisis team personnel

- testing contingency plans and emergency procedures

- dealing with the media

- dealing with victims and their families

- dealing with other affected persons (such as employees)

- getting the organization's normal work done during the crisis

- returning to normal after the crisis (both operationally and in human terms).

As figure 1–1 shows, in the thunderstorm of a crisis it is your umbrella of preparation which keeps you dry. This handbook is designed to assist you in keeping dry by outlining the shape of the crisis management umbrella. The actual construction of the umbrella and how you employ it are matters you must determine. We can only point you in the right directions by identifying what you must do and know, and by giving you a starting point and references. Our suggestions are based on what has occurred in the past. Your situation may differ and you must tailor our suggestions accordingly.

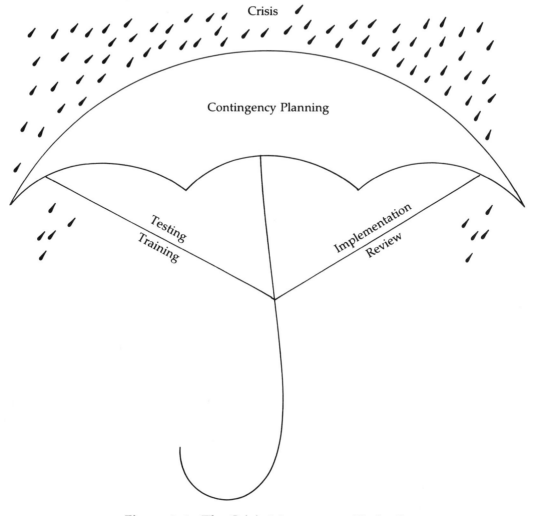

Figure 1–1. The Crisis Management Umbrella

UNDERSTANDING YOUR ORGANIZATION'S POTENTIAL FOR CRISIS:
A CHECKLIST

- ✔ Identify the types of crises to which your organization is exposed.
  Disasters:

  Induced catastrophes:

- ✔ Identify which of your operations, facilities, and/or personnel are at risk.

- ✔ Consider the value of these operations and facilities and what it would cost to replace them to determine how much your organization would lose if they or your personnel were put out of action. Prioritize accordingly.

- ✔ Determine the effect of the various types of possible emergencies on your operations.

- ✔ Identify the broad categories that must be addressed in your contingency planning.

- ✔ Review any existing emergency plans to identify gaps.

- ✔ Consider the environment within which your emergency plans will be implemented. For example, are you dealing with hostility toward your organization or sympathy for its problems? Are you implementing with your own resources exclusively or with the expectation of outside assistance?

ASSESSING THE RISK

2

On August 14, 1969, Hurricane Camille hit the coast of Mississippi, just east
of the Louisiana border. The station at Gulfport registered land speeds for the
hurricane of over one hundred miles per hour with gusts up to 175 mph—an
almost-unheard-of wind speed even for a hurricane. Over the next eight days,
the storm swept all the way through Mississippi and Tennessee as far as Kentucky,
then turned east and ran the full length of Virginia before finally blowing out to
sea. In its wake, it left almost unbelievable damage—storm tides in Mississippi
more than twenty-four feet above sea level, twenty-seven inches of rain dropped
in an eight-hour period in Virginia, severe flash floods, 255 people killed, sixty-
eight missing, and more than a billion dollars in damages.

Hurricanes can be devastating. The combination of tremendous wind speeds and
torrential rainfall, along with the ever-present danger of tornados, floods, and
tidal waves, can destroy vast areas of land, submerge business and residential
areas, even wipe out whole towns. Hurricane Beulah, which struck southern
Texas in September 1967, spawned a record 155 tornados, killing fifteen people
and doing close to have a billion dollars' worth of damage. Hurricane Agnes

swept up the East Coast of the United States from Florida to New York in June 1972, killing 122 people and destroying more than two billion dollars' worth of property—one of the costliest disasters in United States history. Record-breaking river crests were recorded from North Carolina to New York, seventeen tornados were spawned in Florida and Georgia, and massive storm tides buffeted the Florida coast.

The history of hurricane damage in the United States has often been grim. One that swept Galveston Island in the late summer of 1900 killed more than six thousand people. The impossibility of burying them (because the island had been inundated and bodies thrown into the sea kept washing onto shore) eventually led to a serious outbreak of disease. Another hurricane hit southern Florida in 1928, causing the waters of Lake Okeechobee to overflow into the nearby population centers, killing 1,836 people and destroying many millions of dollars' worth of property. Hurricane Audrey, in June 1957, caused Gulf waters to flood across the Louisiana coast as far as twenty-five miles inland, destroying homes and oil installations and killing 381 people.

A hurricane's unpredictability can be as great as its force. Although every major storm up to that time had done its damage in the region of the Gulf, a hurricane hit southern New England on September 10, 1938, killing six hundred people and doing hundreds of millions of dollars' worth of damage before passing north into Canada. Hurricane Donna in 1960 left a trail of devastation from Florida to Canada, killing fifty. Gusts from that storm measured 180 mph in the Florida Keys, 80 mph in Virginia, and 130 mph in Rhode Island.

Any hurricane, even a hurricane warning, is a crisis for those in its path. And its path can be impossible to predict.

A crisis rarely arrives without some kind of warning. Even a disaster normally occurs in an area in which similar phenomena have taken place sometime in the past. Induced catastrophes almost always have some advance indications. A crisis is the point in an emergency where the direction of future events is determined; it is the turning point.[1] That is the reason for contingency planning and crisis management. Were this not the case, there would be no value in advance planning and crisis management would simply be a matter of luck and good guessing.

PRECRISIS ACTIONS

Many emergencies can be prevented completely with adequate thought and action. Others can be anticipated—often by doing nothing more than using common sense. The time for doing this is now, while you still think it won't happen to you. Remember, it wasn't raining when Noah built the ark! That is why governments invest such large amounts of resources in developing information and in translating it into useful intelligence. In any given year, the United States and other governments (along with many corporations) are able to avoid any number of induced catastrophes by taking appropriate actions based upon intelligence, deteriorating conditions in a given area, and similar sorts of early warning indicators. The planning process begins with an understanding of the situation and the recognition that a number of policy decisions must be made before the actual planning can begin. Then, focused planning is carried out in a manner consistent with effective crisis management.[2]

First, let's address the question of how you determine which emergencies apply in a particular situation. By this, we do not mean actual security surveys, threat or risk assessments, or other specific determinations. These are beyond the scope of this handbook. Here, we are discussing only the necessity of determining what disasters or induced catastrophes might apply in a given case.

DISASTERS

There is always some type of record available to guide planners in determining what sorts of natural or accidental emergencies might affect their organizations' operations. Let's look at some of these with a view toward identifying sources of information. (See Appendix B for a fuller listing of sources of information and assistance.)

NATURAL PHENOMENA

Information concerning earthquakes, floods, storms, tidal waves, and other naturally occurring emergencies is available from a number of government and private sources, both domestic and international. On the government side, the U.S. Geological Service, the Federal Emergency Management Agency, the Agency for International Development, the National Oceanic and Atmospheric Administration, the Coast Guard, the Public Health Service, the Centers for Disease Control and many other agencies have historical and statistical information available—sometimes free, sometimes for sale. A glance at any catalog of the U.S. Government Printing Office will provide an amazing breadth of publications on any of these topics. Internationally, many of the agencies of the United Nations (for example, the World Health Organization and its affiliated Pan American Health Organization) and foreign governments have similar data available. On the private side, examples of useful information sources include the Red Cross and independent meteorological services. By taking advantage of these sources of information, not only can the planner increase his or her knowledge concerning disasters generally, he or she can also distill the commonalities and differences among the various types of disaster—thereby enhancing planning abilities. (One often-overlooked potential source of invaluable information is other organizations engaged in operations or business similar to one's own. The "old boy network" can work in various ways—even if you are not an "old boy.") Table 2–1 provides an example of what we mean.

Table 2–1. Short-term Health Effects of Major Natural Disasters

	Earthquake	High winds	Tidal wave/ Flash flood	Flood
Deaths	Many	Few	Many	Few
Severe injuries	Overwhelming	Moderate	Few	Few
Infectious disease	Potential problem in all major disasters			
Food scarcity	Rare	Rare	Common	Common
Dislocations	Rare	Rare	Common	Common

Source: Pan American Health Organization

Some interesting characteristics of major disasters (a few of which are exactly the opposite of the conventional wisdom) include the following:[3]

- Dead bodies are unlikely to become a health hazard after a major disaster.
- Major outbreaks of food-related or water-borne diseases rarely follow natural disasters.
- Large hurricanes produce torrential rainfall; dangerous flooding can occur without warning.
- Hurricanes cause major damage, but deaths are few unless severe flooding occurs.
- In most disasters, the vast majority of injuries will be limited to bruises, cuts, or uncomplicated fractures.
- Earthquakes and volcanic eruptions occur in predictable areas.
- Earthquakes seldom cause nutritional emergencies; floods frequently do.

ACCIDENTS

Accidents are more difficult to plan for given their unexpected occurrence. There is no way to predict which airplane or train will crash, which bridge or building will collapse, or when an industrial accident will occur. However, those of us living near airports or rail lines recognize that, should an air or rail accident occur, we have a greater chance of being involved in it than people not living near these facilities. The same holds true for bridges and buildings. And those of us working in dangerous industries or responsible for the transportation or storage of hazardous materials also should recognize the statistically greater possibility (and, therefore, our greater need to reduce risks wherever possible) of being involved in a major accident.

Nonetheless, there are sources of information available to the contingency planner that can provide considerable information regarding the possibility of accidents, the types of emergencies that might occur, and other data. Among these are local law enforcement and emergency response organizations, hospitals and state/local medical agencies, think tanks, and other consultants. The Federal Aviation Administration publishes a guide to local law enforcement agencies with aviation jurisdictions, which enables planners to coordinate with the appropriate local agencies in this regard. The Federal Emergency Management Agency publishes a variety of manuals dealing with hazardous materials, fallout shelters, transportation, and many other specialized facets of emergency preparedness. (For information regarding how to contact FEMA see Appendix B.)

INDUCED CATASTROPHES

In today's world, no responsible contingency planner can overlook the possibility that his or her organization may become the target of an induced catastrophe—whether for political reasons, criminal reasons, as a result of a labor dispute, or other reasons. Terrorism is the most visible threat to organizations operating internationally. Those whose operations and sources of supply are confined to the United States and Canada would place criminal and other types of manmade threats as more probable than terrorist attack. Yet, other than the motivation of the perpetrators, there is little difference between terrorism and criminal threats: what you do to prepare against the one serves to prepare you for the other as well. Because of this—and because of some aspects particular to acts of terrorism—a brief discussion of the dynamics of terrorism is useful.

Terrorism

The dynamics of terrorism are simple, straightforward, and all-too-often effective. (See figure 2–1.) We will not grapple here with a detailed definition of terrorism beyond noting that it is the threat or use of violence for political purposes.[4]

In reality, terrorism is nothing more than criminal behavior for allegedly political ends. Assassination is no different than murder, hijacking is grand theft, and kidnapping, arson, or bombing remain just that. The only characteristic that distinguishes the terrorist from the common criminal (many of whom are active in terrorist groups) is the self-proclaimed political motivation behind the act.

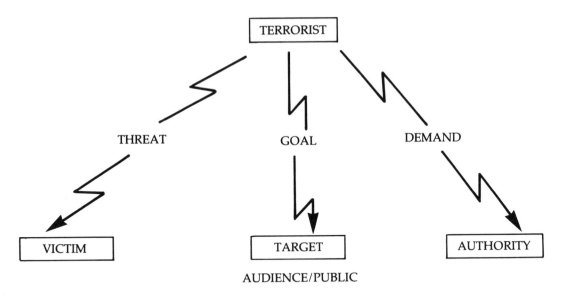

Figure 2–1. The Dynamics of Terrorism

Adapted from the work of Dr. Robert Blum, psychological consultant to the Department of State's Office of Counterterrorism.

The terrorist's political demands are directed against the authorities. In order to exert pressure on them, the terrorist threatens the victim—who is often unable to influence directly the authority's action, but whose predicament at once provides the terrorist with leverage and the authority with a reason to deal with the terrorist. The terrorist's goal is to accomplish this in an attention-getting manner to publicize his or her political views. Often the terrorist is successful. World leaders paid little attention to Northern Ireland or the demands of Palestinians until the Irish Republican Army and the Palestine Liberation Organization attracted media attention through a spate of bombings and hijackings.

It is this political motivation that places terrorism in a category of its own and makes it so difficult to handle. Political violence has long been accepted by nations as a unique manifestation of the struggle for self-determination. For that reason, most extradition treaties continue to exclude political crimes from their provisions. Today's terrorists, however, have gone far beyond the nineteenth century self-imposed limitations on their activities that made such violence tolerable. Additionally, countries have discovered terrorism to be a low-cost, low-risk method of attacking their enemies.

Terrorists no longer limit their attacks to the source of perceived political abuses or its direct agents. Terrorists can—and do—attack anything from airplanes to restaurants to boats. Governments cannot protect every possible target against every possible kind of attack. Innocent bystanders—formerly off limits—are frequently the most immediate victims of terrorist attacks, often for no more reason than their being in the wrong place at the wrong time.

Terrorism is not mindless, random violence. It is calculated and focused to achieve its perpetrator's goals in striking at a vulnerable target in a way designed to attract maximum attention with minimal risk (except, of course, in those relatively few instances in which the terrorist intends to die).

CRIMINAL ACTS

Security specialists and planners have long attempted to cope with the various manifestations of criminal activity that could affect their organization's operations and the safety of personnel. Terrorism is but another example of this phenomenon. Extortion, bombings, arson, theft, assault, and other threats are well-known and require no enumeration here. For our purposes, it is sufficient to note that they are a subcategory of induced catastrophes.

DISRUPTIVE ACTIONS

Strikes, demonstrations, and other actions can result in the disruption of normal operations of an organization even if they are peaceful and orderly. However, intentionally or otherwise, these types of actions can get out of hand and result in damage to facilities, and/or possible injury or death to your personnel (those charged with security precautions for the 1988 Summer Olympics in Seoul, Korea have had pointed reminders of this). Many otherwise unexplained events have proved to be the work of disgruntled employees or other "insiders"—a factor that must always remain in the mind of a contingency planner or security specialist. Also falling in this subcategory (although here, as in other cases, there can be an overlap with other subcategories) would be instances of product tampering, contamination, and sabotage.

Two recent and particularly unpleasant examples of this sort of problem have happened in the past few years. In one case, the teenage son of a State Department employee sneaked a gun into the State Department building and killed his mother, for purely personal reasons. As it happened, she worked on the same floor as the Secretary of State, inadvertently pointing up how easy it would have been for this domestic disturbance to have become instead an assassination. In another instance, a recently dismissed employee of Pacific Southwest Airlines used his old identification to smuggle a gun aboard a flight his former boss was taking, resulting in the crash of the plane and the death of forty-three passengers. Both cases led to revisions in security procedures, but too late to do anything for the victims of these attacks.

Regardless of the subcategory of induced catastrophe, such emergencies rarely occur out of a clear sky. Areas of terrorist activity are continually tracked by governments and private firms. Law enforcement agencies around the world maintain records about criminal activity within their jurisdictions. With minimal effort, planners can determine what disruptive events might affect their organizations.

PROACTIVE CRISIS MANAGEMENT

The term "crisis management" has become quite popular in recent years. It is used for everything from responding to family disputes to dealing with acts of terrorism. Unfortunately, most of what passes for crisis management is *reactive* and *ad hoc*. Often, there is little advance planning, or what planning there is consists of untested assumptions filed away someplace until an emergency occurs. This is precisely what crisis management should not be. Our contention is that effective planning should include proactive mechanisms that have been tested and revised over time and that can be implemented by personnel who are carefully selected, properly trained, and secure in their authority and procedures.

DEVELOPING A CRISIS ACTION PLAN: A CHECKLIST

- ✔ Identify the types of disasters/induced catastrophes that have occurred in your area of operations.

- ✔ Identify those that could affect your operations in the future.

- ✔ In the case of induced catastrophes, determine which scenarios are plausible.

- ✔ Survey your physical facilities and operating procedures to determine your preparedness for any emergency that could affect your organization's operations.

- ✔ Survey the surrounding area to determine if there are operations or facilities near you whose activities might create emergencies that could affect you. For example: airports, governmental/military facilities, industrial facilities, hazardous waste dumps, railroads, pipelines.

- ✔ Establish liaison with local law enforcement agencies, local/national governmental agencies, local emergency response agencies and hospitals, Red Cross, private specialists, and other groups with concerns similar to yours. (See Appendix B.)

✔ Know where to get help, how to get help, what help you can expect, and how long it will take help to arrive from law enforcement agencies, local/state/federal government agencies, consultants, private security companies, disaster relief agencies, medical response facilities, and so forth.

✔ Identify the specialists you will require for various contingencies and establish relationships and procedures with them.

✔ Determine the status of your insurance policies. Are they adequate? Know what restrictions exist and what procedures must be followed to ensure your coverage is valid.

✔ Know who currently has authority to make key decisions within your organization and who controls access to the decision-maker(s) in an emergency.

✔ Review any existing emergency guidance and ensure its completeness and accuracy.

✔ Review any procedures your organization now has and identify any gaps or inaccuracies.

THE ELEMENTS OF EFFECTIVE CRISIS MANAGEMENT

3

On August 7, 1982, several dozen airline passengers were sitting in the international flight departure area of Esenboga International Airport in Ankara, Turkey, waiting for their next flight to be called. Like passengers in transit all over the world, they were passing the time in the usual ways: reading, sipping coffee, and checking the airline schedules to be sure their next flight was still on time. Suddenly, two gunmen rushed into the departure area, fired a submachinegun at random into the crowd, and set off a bomb. What had been a normal, peaceful summer day was turned into a scene of carnage.

The Armenian Secret Army for the Liberation of Armenia (ASALA) had dedicated itself to seeking revenge against Turkey for events that took place during World War I and to the carving out of an autonomous Armenia from Turkish territory. This quest has included assassinations of Turkish diplomats, takeovers of embassies, and numerous bombings. The Esenboga attack set new levels of viciousness, as its victims had no connection with Turkey or Turkish history.

As the smoke cleared from the explosion, police returned the terrorists' fire and managed to capture one of them. The other fled to the airport restaurant, where he took fifteen or twenty people hostage. When one woman tried to escape, he shot and killed her. Police tried to talk him into surrendering, but he refused, setting off another bomb in the restaurant. The police then had no choice but to attack. In the hail of bullets that followed, many people were badly hurt before the terrorist was finally killed. In a little less than two hours, seventy-one people were injured, nine were killed, and Esenboga Airport resembled a battlefield.

Those eighty people had little or no interest in the problems of the region. They were just waiting for a plane.

Crisis management has become a buzzword in government and industry. Much has been written and said about it, but little of the commentary has been proactive. Whether in government or the private sector, crisis management generally consists of some sort of plan (often rudimentary, untested, and out of date), the identification of some chain of command for decision-making (consisting of personnel who are often uninvolved in the plan's preparation, untrained in emergency procedures, and unused to the stresses of crises), and little more than a guess regarding the resources and mechanisms required to cope with the emergency. Contemporary crisis management, in short, is often little more than "rolling with the punches" and hoping for the best. In one of the great understatements of all time, and perhaps as a warning to everyone else, *Fortune* magazine commented in the wake of the Bhopal tragedy that "[Union] Carbide lacked a pre-existing corporate plan for coping with a catastrophe of this magnitude."[1] In truth, though, so do many other organizations which should by now know better.

In most organizations, crisis management and contingency planning develops along the same general lines as most other projects. Figure 3–1 depicts these stages.

Stage 1: Enthusiasm
Stage 2: Disillusionment/Confusion
Stage 3: Search for the Guilty
Stage 4: Punishment of the Innocent
Stage 5: Reward of the Uninvolved

Figure 3–1. The Stages of any Project

Although tongue-in-cheek, we would like to demonstrate figure 3–1's applicability to the incorrect style of crisis management.

In many organizations, the idea that some type of emergency will occur gets little consideration. Most governmental agencies and many large corporations recognize that such situations do occur, but the press of everyday requirements mitigates the amount of time and thought devoted to consideration of such eventualities. In Stage 1, the task of emergency planning often is delegated to a middle- to junior-level functionary. Generally, this person is overworked, but enthusiastically accepts this additional responsibility because he or she (a) has no other choice, (b) recognizes the importance of planning for these contingencies, (c) realizes that, in the event of an emergency, career advancement will weigh in the balance. Pick as many as apply.

For a period of time, all goes well, as our planner works alone outlining the scope of the plan, identifying the informational requirements and the questions that must be encompassed, and, in general, laying the groundwork for the plan itself. At some point, he or she requires the assistance of other personnel who have specialized knowledge relevant to some facet of the plan or whose seniority is sufficient to make a decision concerning the plan. But the planner discovers that no one has any time to devote to this matter. After all, the planner was delegated this task in order to free others to do the important work of the organization's daily business. Soon the planner realizes that he or she will have to do the best job possible without much, if any, help from anyone else. Stage 2 ensues as the planner begins to see the task as a thankless one in which he or she must develop a lot of information about unfamiliar matters in the absence of any guidance from senior management.

The planner assembles the most comprehensive plan possible under the circumstances. This plan is then copied, distributed as appropriate, and filed away by each recipient. Those who take the time to read it make no comments on its adequacy or completeness and, eventually, move on to other positions. Most recipients don't even read it. The plan sits in a file drawer, unread, untested, and unupdated. Eventually an emergency happens and the plan is dusted off and used.

As happens in even the best-prepared organization, not everything goes perfectly during the emergency. In fact, a couple of important mistakes are made and the public image of the organization suffers. Even before things completely return to normal, senior management wants to know why. Stage 3 commences with the formation of a special committee to investigate the organization's response to the emergency. Our planner writes a number of memoranda and attends several meetings to explain why the emergency was allowed to occur and why the plan was inadequate.

Stage 4 follows quickly on the heels on Stage 3. Our planner's reputation suffers as the result of the organization's shooting itself in the foot. While the planner's job security does not suffer, career advancement has been capped well below what might have been. Finally, to demonstrate to the world that the organization really did do a good job of responding to the emergency, our planner's superiors (all of whom were to busy to help develop the plan, read it and comment upon its completeness, or to participate in testing it) receive some combination of bonuses, promotions, and public acclaim. Stage 5 has been reached. (This is a perennial problem for the State Department. Embassies frequently submit emergency action plans that are incomplete and/or outdated. A partial solution to this was the creation of State's Crisis Management Exercise Program, of which more will be said later.)

PROACTIVE CRISIS MANAGEMENT

We contend that *true* crisis management is more than reflexes and luck. While in many ways it is *reactively* oriented, *effective* crisis management is a collection of *anticipatory* measures that enable an organization to coordinate and control its responses to an emergency. Remember that a crisis is the turning point of any emergency. Effective crisis management permits an organization to maximize its opportunities and minimize the dangers it confronts. Having a well-considered, well-tested contingency plan is important, but the planning process must occur within the nourishing ambience of effective, proactive crisis management. By nourishment we mean, among other things, the willingness of senior management to make policy decisions that determine the direction(s) the planners will take. We will discuss these policy decisions in chapter 4.

We believe the best crisis managers are those who are also involved in the contingency planning process that should precede any emergency, as one of us pointed out to Canada's Olympic Integrated Intelligence Unit during the preparations for the 1988 Winter Olympics in Calgary. Ideally, the impetus of Stage 1 can be maintained throughout the planning process, reducing Stage 2's delays and inaccuracies. If properly executed, proactive crisis management should eliminate Stages 3 and 4 and convert Stage 5 into an organizational lovefest.

AN OVERVIEW OF CRISIS MANAGEMENT

Crisis managers deserving of the title must be prepared to do a number of things. These will be discussed in detail in chapter 5, but a brief overview will be useful now. Figure 3–2 depicts the eight basic elements of effective, proactive crisis management.

Like any construction project, the pyramid requires a solid foundation. The basis of the crisis management pyramid is senior management's willingness to *think about the unpopular*. There must be a clear recognition that emergencies of various types are distinct possibilities and that preparations for them must begin *now*— well in advance of their occurrence. However small the probability of such events, they can occur and, if not prepared for, they will have devastating results.

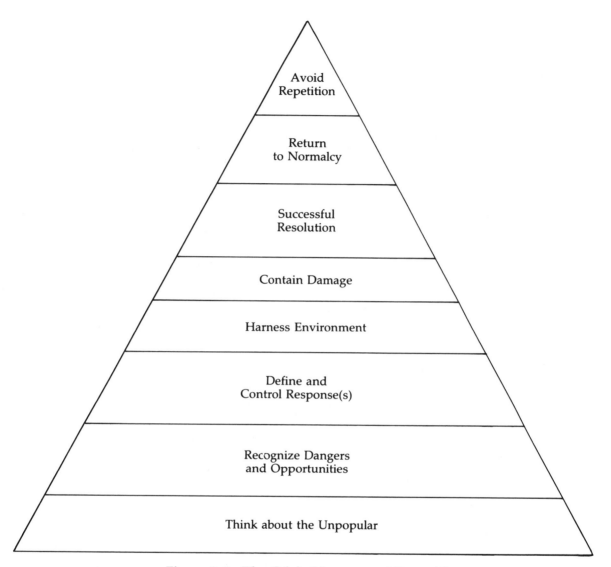

Figure 3–2. The Crisis Management Pyramid

This is easier said than done. Many times, the press of everyday events and responsibilities makes it difficult to focus on the unpredictable. And emergencies *are* unpredictable. Additionally, senior management often falls victim to the fallacy that devoting time to considering such low-probability events is a waste of the organization's most valuable resource, the time of senior management. In this view, the managerial skills of senior management are better spent by focusing on sales, services, quality assurance, or other profit-making (in the case of a private firm) or bureaucratic (in the case of a government agency) tasks.

Therefore, the first requirement for effective crisis management is recognizing that the involvement of senior management is essential at the earliest stages of the contingency planning process. The relatively minor demands on the time and attention of senior management at this stage will pay large dividends when the crisis arrives.

Only through this recognition is the second building block of the pyramid supported: *recognition of dangers and opportunities.* When the crisis arrives, it will often be surrounded by a plethora of details and diversions. Determining the significance of problems will be difficult. This process is immeasurably aided if the crisis managers have been actively involved during planning. As will be discussed later, the job of the crisis manager is to focus on the important matters during the crisis, to distinguish the opportunities from the dangers, and to ensure that the proper steps are taken.

This requires the *defining and control of crisis response(s).* As Aesop wrote many centuries ago, "to do the right thing at the right season is a great art." Such greatness does not come by accident. It is the product of common sense, training, good planning, and good luck. But in this case, when luck arrives, it merely enhances the actions of the successful crisis manager; it does not determine them.

Definition of the response is the product of preparation, but controlling it requires that crisis managers *harness the environment.* This is not as promethean a task as it sounds. It requires a willingness to delegate, an ability to organize, and a humane appreciation of the stresses encountered in any emergency situation. Above all, harnessing the environment means providing an atmosphere in which your personnel can do the jobs for which they were selected. It means providing the right facilities, scheduling shifts, and providing backups, and adding the figurative pat on the back when appropriate. Chapter 5 discusses this in more detail.

The next block in the pyramid is almost self-evident. A major function of crisis management is to *contain the damage* to your organization. Physical damage frequently is impossible to control, but emotional and public relations damage is not. The same humane appreciation that is so important in managing the crisis is equally important in coping with the not-always-visible damage. Chapter 8 discusses some often-overlooked aspects of this damage. As for public relations, chapter 7 will give you our views on how effective crisis management can win the battle for the hearts and minds of the public and, in so doing, garner support and appreciation for your organization from the public and your own employees.

If you are successful in containing damage, you will have advanced considerably toward your next objective: *successful resolution* of the emergency. The measure of success will vary with the emergency, but it always entails emerging from the crisis in as nearly identical a position as before the crisis. In some cases, it may even be possible to emerge in a better position. Each type of emergency presents its own challenges, but your objective remains the same.

Your next task as a crisis manager is to *return to normalcy*. Whatever this means in terms of your organization's activities, planning for an orderly resumption of normal operations is often left to chance. In human terms, this means the crisis manager must oversee the assistance victims might require. In facility terms, it means someone must ensure that equipment is safe to operate and buildings are safe to enter. A complex production process (built up over many years) cannot simply be restarted by flipping a switch. The successful crisis manager will have ensured that the planning process has addressed—and tested—this facet of the emergency.

Finally, and in many ways most important, you must find ways to *avoid repetition* of the incident. Disasters can rarely be prevented; they can, however, often be mitigated. Induced catastrophes frequently can be prevented through more aggressive countermeasures. Your analysis of the emergency—from warning signs, if any (the prodromal or precrisis stage), to its resolution—will provide you with valuable lessons. You can use these to reduce your vulnerability to similar emergencies in the future.

To conclude this chapter, let us review the highlights of effective crisis management depicted in figure 3–3. We have already discussed several of them. The balance will be discussed in detail elsewhere.

Good Planning
- Consider *all* possibilities.
- Don't focus only on immediate problems.
- Establish your contacts *now*.

Good Personnel
- Look for experience and knowledge.
- Train, test, and evaluate.
- Use people effectively and humanely.
- Organize to mitigate stress.

Good Shakedowns
- Test plans and people.
- Evaluate and revise plans.
- *Keep an open mind.*

Maintain Control
- Stay ahead of the flow.
- Schedule/pace yourself.
- Look for the *real* problems.
- Be creative.
- Retain public affairs initiative.
- Rely on your people.
- Have confidence in your plan.
- Keep records.

Get Back to Normal
- Evaluate and document.
- Reward.
- Analyze implications.

Figure 3–3. The Key Components of Crisis Management

REVIEWING YOUR CRISIS ACTION PLAN: A CHECKLIST

✔ Review your emergency action plan to determine its completeness.

✔ Test your plan to identify areas where it should be updated, then retest it.

✔ Determine the chain of command in an emergency and ensure that each link in the chain is aware of its role, responsibilities, and authority.

✔ Ensure that each employee reads the plan.

✔ Identify the resources the plan requires and check to see that they are available and in working order.

✔ Determine what resources are required to test the plan and obtain them.

✔ Structure the plan review to ensure the involvement of:
  • senior management
  • relevant section heads
  • emergency team members
  • other employees
  • outside specialists and other organizations, as appropriate

✔ Be certain *all* elements of the crisis management pyramid are contained in your plan.

POLICY ISSUES IN CRISIS PLANNING

4

Gordon Wilson said he asked his daughter four times how she was and each time she replied that she was all right.

"I asked her the fifth time and she said, 'Daddy, I love you very much.' Those were her last words," Wilson, sobbing, told reporters. His daughter was one of eleven people—all civilians—killed by the explosion of a terrorist bomb on a peaceful Sunday afternoon, November 8, 1987, in Enniskillen, Northern Ireland.

The explosion had not been a loud one, Wilson said, and although he and his daughter had been buried under the rubble of a building, he had thought that no one had been badly injured. "I then felt somebody holding my hand quite firmly. It was Marie and she said, 'Are you all right, Daddy?' I said 'yes.' "

The following day, the Irish Republican Army admitted placing the bomb at the town memorial in honor of the United Kingdom's war dead. It apologized for the

Portions of this chapter appeared for the first time in two articles published in the IACP's *Clandestine Tactics and Technology* series. See notes 2 and 3.

death of the eleven people, stating that the bomb had been intended to kill British soldiers during a parade and wreath-laying ceremony, but it had exploded prematurely.[1]

The 1980s have frequently been referred to as the most litigious period in the history of the United States. It appears that individuals and organizations are taken into court for the smallest mistake—whether of commission or omission. Indeed, there have been instances where corporations have been sued by stockholders, employees, and others over the manner in which they responded to terrorist crises.[2] Regardless of the type of emergency, organizations that neglect advance preparations risk becoming targets of lawsuits. And, should the emergency prove to have been avoidable or, if unavoidable, mishandled, then the ramifications of such lawsuits, coupled with considerable adverse publicity, can trouble the organization for years after the event.[3] As we have written before:

Contingency planning is the essential action which permits a company to maximize the effectiveness of its response to a crisis and, hence, the likelihood of success in dealing with it. Every corporation will eventually face some type of crisis—whether it is terrorism, natural disaster, or some other. It is advisable to consider such crises before the fact and to prepare accordingly.[4]

POLICIES AND PRIORITIES

Before any serious planning can be done, the framework and parameters for the plan must be established. This requires drawing up organizational policies and priorities, which provide the guidance the planners will require to develop effective contingency plans. Because crisis decisions often must be made quickly, the more detailed and comprehensive the contingency planning, the easier the decision-making process. The purpose of such planning is to have as many decisions as possible already made and ready for implementation. To do so requires clear guidance in the form of organizational policies and priorities.

Policies and priorities go hand in hand. Determining the former requires you to delineate the latter. Let us now turn to the basic policy issues for emergency planning and action, as depicted in figure 4–1.

It is extremely important that the organization define its policies and priorities within the context of the governmental policies that surround any emergency. Unless your organization *is* a governmental agency, then you must ensure that you are not selecting policies that will conflict with the government (whether state, local, federal, or foreign). Even if you represent a governmental agency or a military entity, you must ensure that your policies and priorities do not conflict with those of other agencies or a higher authority in your chain of command. Among the questions you must consider are:

- In an induced catastrophe such as a terrorist incident, what can be negotiated and in what manner?

- In a disaster such as a flood or earthquake, what relief supplies can be released and through what procedures?

Coordination of Organizational and Governmental Policies.
Who/What Will Receive What Kind/How Much of Effort?
How Will Contact with the Public be Handled?
How Will Policies be Communicated?
Who Will be in Charge of What?
What Should be Codified?
Chain of Command/Extent of Authority.
Distribution of Information.
Organizational Responses: Hard or Soft?
Access to Sensitive Information.
Media Contacts: By Whom and How.
Role of Outsiders.
Training of Personnel/Exercises.
Archival Requirements/Documentation.

Figure 4–1. Policy Issues for Crisis Planning

An extremely important facet of emergency planning is often overlooked until the crisis has arrived, namely, who and what are to be included in the organization's response? This can be a difficult question, especially if left until too late. Organizations are frequently surprised to learn there are at least twenty-two categories of people who might look to the organization for assistance in an emergency.[5] An organization will recognize the wisdom of deciding in advance just how far it feels an obligation to undertake responsibility for emergency responses. Included among the considerations are: key personnel versus non-key personnel, citizenship of employees, full-time versus part-time employees, whether the damage is the fault of the company, and the person's affiliation with the organization.

Another important issue is how to deal with the public. This matter is often given only cursory consideration during the contingency planning stage. This function is broader than the media relations or public affairs role. It also includes dealing with victims, family members, and organization employees, for example. There are many considerations for performing this function, which is distinct and separate from dealing with the media. Chapter 8 discusses victims and other affected persons and the considerations elaborated therein should be taken into account during the policy-making and planning phases of the emergency planning cycle.

The next issue is delegation of duties. The emergency chain of command, which may differ considerably from the routine hierarchy, must be made clear. Chapter 5 details a number of important facets of selecting and organizing a Crisis Action Team. However yours is organized, you must be certain that everyone clearly understands his or her responsibilities and the limits of his or her authority. Responsibility without authority is almost meaningless in effective crisis management.[6]

The next two points are related: How will policies be communicated? What should be codified? Formulating policies is of little value unless they are known by all. How else can compliance be expected and/or enforced? One of the easiest ways to distribute policy decisions to all employees, family members, and anyone else who should be aware of them is through memoranda, press releases, and other documents. This is really codification of policy and it should be done as quickly as possible to ensure that it has been understood in advance of any emergency. These key policy documents should also be incorporated into the emergency plan itself to ensure that the planning document is a complete and ready reference in time of need.

Another policy that must be decided is the philosophy of information release during a crisis. By this we mean a conscious decision about the priority and fullness of information to be provided. Is the organization primarily concerned with ensuring the full and timely flow of information only to itself, or does it see an obligation to keep the public at large continuously informed? The answer to this question will determine the public affairs and other tactics employed during the emergency. Our recommendation is that, in almost every case, an organization is best served by a policy of disclosure of information to the public at large, along with its internal disclosures—subject, of course, to legal and common-sense restraints. Chapter 7 discusses at length the various facets of an effective and open public affairs approach to crisis management.

The organization's responses to induced catastrophes such as terrorism and criminal extortion also must be determined beforehand. Will the organization consider the payment of ransoms or other concessions or will it adopt a firm no-concessions stance? (See Appendix C for a brief discussion of one aspect of ransom payments.) This decision, in turn, will affect a range of planning matters, such as whether to purchase kidnap and ransom insurance and the establishment of special financial arrangements. Above all, the organization's management must understand the policies of the various government agencies (both domestic and international) with which their decisions and organizational interests may conflict and the likely responses of those agencies.

One aspect of contingency planning is the crisis managers' access to sensitive information during an emergency. It is not unknown for governments to share intelligence information with private organizations and individuals when appropriate; however, the appropriateness often is defined in terms of the compatibility of the private organization's approach to the situation with governmental policies and procedures. Should it become necessary, is the organization able to and prepared to seek out other sources for such information? If the answer is no, then everyone should know that in advance.

Elsewhere (chapter 7), we discuss in some detail our philosophy and approach to the question of media relations. For the organizational policy-makers, the question at this point is who will handle this task and in what fashion? Remember, no matter how well an organization handles an emergency, if the public image is negative, the organization will be perceived as incompetent, inconsiderate, and unsuccessful.

No organization should plan for emergencies without considering the use of outside specialists or consultants. This is not essential if the organization has in-house expertise in all facets of planning, crisis management, and recovery. However, few organizations outside of government enjoy such a luxury. At the same time, senior management should make clear by means of a policy decision that the use of appropriate outside assistance in training, planning, or other needed areas is acceptable and will in no way reflect adversely upon the career progression of anyone within the organization. Managers or others within an organization often fear they will be penalized if they admit to a need or desire for outside assistance in any area within their responsibility. This fear is often grounded in a reluctance to devote extra resources to functions that do not translate into quantifiable profit-and-loss terms. We have met with hundreds of corporate security officers laboring under this handicap.

This philosophy can affect the organization's approach to the training of personnel and the evaluation of emergency plans. This is another area in which an organizational policy is essential. If senior management recognizes the importance of the proper selection of personnel, the proper training for these personnel, and the frequent updating of plans and procedures, the organization will acquit itself well during an emergency. Such management will support and participate in the training and exercise programs designed for this purpose. (See chapter 9 about exercises.)

Finally, it is important to keep records of each step along the planning path and each action taken during an emergency. This is important for a number of reasons, including the ability to defend the organization against legal action of any sort and the ability to learn from past actions in planning for emergencies. The organization's senior management must establish a clear policy on this so that proper procedures, forms, and training can be implemented.[7]

Having established the background against which the planning for emergencies can take place, let us turn to the question of selecting the Crisis Action Team. After all, it is extremely important to be sure that the right people are on the team, because they are the ones who run the show.

REVIEWING POLICIES, PROCEDURES, AND PLANS: A CHECKLIST

- ✔ Compile and review your organization's policies on various contingencies before establishing your plans.

- ✔ Ensure that these policies are known throughout the organization and that they are included in your emergency manuals.

- ✔ Ensure that your procedures and plans are consistent with your organization's established policies and goals.

- ✔ Ensure that your organization's policies are as consistent as possible with the policies and procedures of the government(s) and any other organization(s) with which you might have to work during an emergency.

- ✔ Identify appropriate outside consultants and other sources of assistance in developing and implementing your plans and procedures.

- ✔ Ensure that appropriate personnel have any security clearances or background checks which might be required.

- ✔ Establish a viable record-keeping and archival system and procedures to ensure they are followed.

ORGANIZING YOUR CRISIS ACTION TEAM

5

In 1960, McNeil Consumer Products Company, a division of Johnson & Johnson, received permission from the Food and Drug Administration to market its new Tylenol tablet for use without a prescription. Fifteen years later, in 1975, the company introduced Extra-Strength Tylenol capsules and began advertising directly to consumers (previously the drug had been promoted only to the medical community). By August 1982, Tylenol had captured over 35 percent of the market and was outselling the next four of its competitors combined. Profits were phenomenal and the future was unlimited.

Then the roof fell in.

On the morning of September 30, 1982, it was announced that the recent deaths of three people in Chicago had been traced to Extra-Strength Tylenol capsules

Portions of this chapter previously appeared in Antokol and Nudell, "Generic Contingency Planning for Terrorist Incidents," *Clandestine Tactics and Technology*, vol. 11: issue 8, copyright 1984 by Norman Antokol and Mayer Nudell.

that contained cyanide. The story rocketed through the media. Within the first week of the crisis, it is estimated that more than 90 percent of the American people knew about the deaths and their connection to the poisoned Tylenol capsules. After about two weeks, that figure was 99 percent. More than eighty thousand news stories appeared across the nation, hundreds of hours of radio and television broadcasting were given to the story, and millions of people were gripped with fear. Some suggested that terrorism, in a completely unanticipated form, had come to America.

By the middle of October, copycat crimes were appearing all over the United States. Although the cases involving Tylenol were confined to the Chicago area and the actual death toll was very low, Tylenol was inevitably mentioned in news stories about contaminated medications. The FDA made it clear that neither McNeil nor Johnson & Johnson were in any way at fault, but hysteria swept the country. Tylenol's 35 percent share of the market fell dramatically to less than 7 percent. McNeil and its parent company were in serious trouble.

The company's response was a textbook example of crisis management. All Tylenol advertising was suspended and thirty-one million bottles of Tylenol capsules were withdrawn from stores and destroyed. Consumers were given refunds for the bottles they returned. The company tested another eight million individual capsules, finding in the process that only eight bottles had actually been tampered with. Corporate executives made themselves available to the media and put the reputation of Johnson & Johnson behind the product. A toll-free consumer hotline was established and the company produced videotapes and organized personal appearances by senior executives. Each and every consumer inquiry was answered and consumer studies were undertaken to learn firsthand of public perceptions of the company and the emergency.

Once the actual crisis was over, Johnson & Johnson was left with the problem of picking up the pieces. Many outside the company felt Tylenol was finished, but a national sales meeting was held November 9, at which the commitment to rebuild was announced. Two days later, a national news conference was held to unveil new, triple–safety–sealed packaging. Free coupons were offered to replace Tylenol supplies that people had discarded during the panic. Using satellite transmission, the company reached six hundred reporters in thirty cities around the country, besides offering a direct videofeed of the news conference to all U.S. television stations. McNeil executives began making numerous appearances on local television and radio shows, and a new advertising campaign was begun in January 1983, emphasizing the new safety packaging and the work done on Tylenol to regain the public trust.

Although these steps cost the company about one hundred million dollars, the return was tremendous. Johnson & Johnson and McNeil received widespread praise for the promptness and integrity with which it handled the crisis. And in a very short time, Tylenol had regained nearly all the ground lost in the original panic.

The successful recovery was the result of an awareness of the jobs that needed to be done, the right people assigned to do them, openness with the media, and concern for the affected parties. Johnson & Johnson, through effective crisis management, had turned an induced catastrophe into a public relations triumph.

An emergency plan is only as good as the people who create it and the people who implement it. Your Crisis Action Team should be part of the former, as well as performing the latter function. If not, you risk disconnections between your organization's policies and their implementation. Therefore, the selection of your Crisis Action Team is an extremely important matter. Effective crisis management is largely a matter of leadership and organization. In an emergency, your organization will be required to make a number of time-sensitive decisions to implement critical portions of your emergency plans. The ability to do so decisively and efficiently is all-important.

CRISIS TEAM LEADERSHIP

Leadership of your Crisis Action Team must be vested in one person, who should designate an alternate capable of acting independently in his or her absence. One of the team leader's primary tasks is to ensure that control is maintained over the team's activities, information flow, and the implementation of decisions and organizational policies.

For these reasons, the team leader should be a person who has demonstrated the ability to function under pressure and who has sufficient experience to enjoy the confidence of your organization's most-senior management. While rank within your organizational hierarchy need not be the decisive factor in selection of the leader, he or she must have sufficient authority to make on-the-spot decisions within the framework of overall organization policy, access to top decision-makers when required, and the ability to recognize which decisions to make independently and which to refer to upper management.

Additionally, the team leader (along with the alternate leader) should be closely involved in the selection of the other members of the Crisis Action Team and should ensure that all team members and *their* alternates are thoroughly familiar with the emergency plan well in advance of any incident. The team leader also should conduct periodic reviews of the plan and procedures with other team members to ensure that all key personnel remain conversant with their responsibilities.

FUNCTIONAL REQUIREMENTS FOR CRISIS ACTION TEAMS

Each crisis will differ in some fashion as to its effect on your organization and, therefore, the requirements imposed upon your Crisis Action Team. However, as we have discussed earlier, there are sufficient commonalities in *all* types of emergencies and crises to permit the identification of the *minimum* demands placed upon your Crisis Action Team. (We know this because, at one time or another, we have performed most of these tasks and worked closely with specialists performing the others.) Figure 5–1 lists these functional requirements. All of these will be required; however, depending on circumstances, the number of people required to perform these tasks may vary. These functional commonalities will apply to any internationally operating organization, whether governmental or private, and the Crisis Action Team's effectiveness will depend on having established these requirements in the emergency plan.

We have already discussed some of the functions of the team leader and the alternate team leader. At this point, we would like to review briefly the balance of figure 5–1, moving then to a discussion of the Crisis Action Team's roles before, during, and after an emergency.

As in any organization, the Crisis Action Team leader must have an able executive assistant to ensure that decisions are carried out appropriately and to keep track of the flow of operations. This executive assistance is like an appendage of the team leader's body and must be able to perform likewise for the alternate team leader. It is the executive assistant who will ensure that deadlines are met, promises kept, and decisions implemented.

Another key player on the Crisis Action Team is the person assigned the public affairs role. This role is so important in our view that we have devoted all of chapter 7 to a discussion of our views on this matter. At this point, we would like to stress that the public affairs person—the spokesperson—must enjoy the confidence of the team leader/alternate in order to be effective. It is not an easy task, but it is the most visible and, in many ways, one of the most important tasks of effective crisis management. Keeping the public affairs person fully informed and involved is crucial. After the January 1986 mid-air explosion of the space shuttle *Challenger*, NASA's reputation suffered more than was necessary when a prolonged period of time elapsed between the worldwide live television coverage of the tragedy and the appearance of a NASA official to talk about what had happened to the crew. Despite the fact that the world had witnessed the explosion, this official was unable to add anything to what was already known.

The security liaison role is wide-ranging and not confined to ensuring that no one walks off with organizational property. Among the important liaison functions this person performs (in addition to supervising the organization's own

Team Leader/Alternate

Executive Assistant

Public Affairs

Security Liaison

Governmental Liaison

Administrative Support

Rumor Control

Communications Specialist

Legal Specialist

Financial Specialist

Relief Operations Liaison

Medical Liaison

Victim/Family Liaison

Incident Site Liaison

International Liaison

Figure 5–1. Crisis Action Team Members

security response to the emergency) are: contacts with police and fire agencies that may become involved in responding to the emergency; contacts with any outside private security firms or consultants the organization may require; remaining abreast of tactical developments that might affect the organization's personnel and/or facilities; and, where possible, remaining in touch with intelligence agencies.

Governmental liaison is also a wide-ranging effort. It encompasses not only civilian agencies, but also military ones as appropriate. The person assigned this task must establish and remain in close, continuing contact with local, state, and federal agencies, as well as with international organizations and governments when needed. On occasion, this person may be better suited to maintain or supplement some of the intelligence or other liaisons of the security team member.

Administrative support is an important function frequently overlooked until an emergency occurs. The person in charge of administration must ensure that appropriate numbers and kinds of support personnel are available when needed. In addition, the correct kinds of supplies must either be on hand or immediately available to the Crisis Action Team. This role also includes ensuring that the Crisis Management Center (see next chapter) is properly equipped and serviceable in accordance with the requirements of the Crisis Action Team. This team member also must see that appropriate linguistic support is available as needed. Not only must you be certain that you have this support, but it must be dependable. During the planning for the 1988 Winter Olympics, it was learned that the most immediately available interpreter of a particular language was viewed by some government officials as a security risk. Additionally, this person ensures that the approved procedures for the functioning of the Crisis Action Team and its support personnel are followed.

Rumor control is another frequently overlooked duty, which can be of crucial importance to the success or failure of the organization's crisis management efforts. It is too often confused with the overall public affairs effort, but this is not correct. Rumor control is employed by the Crisis Action Team to identify and correct false information *before* it becomes a public affairs problem. This is done on several levels. First, the rumor control person is in close contact with the organization's other employees—those who are not victims of the emergency or directly engaged in the crisis management efforts. Second, rumor control works closely with the victim/family liaison. Finally, rumor control works with public affairs. The focus is to ensure that all interested parties have a point to contact for information.

Communications are an essential part of crisis management. Information must flow to the Crisis Action Team and from the team to the media, the organization, victims' families, and others. In an international emergency, these communications must often flow in various languages and through various means, ranging from telephone to data transmission to telegrams. Without an adequate flow of information to and from the Crisis Action Team, effective crisis management is impossible. A specialist in the technical side of communications should be part of the Crisis Action Team in all three phases of an emergency: planning, response, and recovery.

Legal advice is always helpful in an emergency. Remember that you are dealing with an extraordinary situation. Whether or not you have anticipated the occurrence of a particular emergency, you are well-advised to have available to you competent legal counsel. (Think back to note 2 in chapter 4.) Today's decisions may become tomorrow's litigation.[1] Legal help during the planning phase may help you to avoid pitfalls experienced by other organizations. This is not to say that your organization's legal adviser must be present in the Crisis Management Center continuously; rather, that such advice be available and used by the Crisis Action Team.

A financial specialist should also be available to the Crisis Action Team leader. Depending on the type of emergency with which your organization is attempting to cope, you may need to obtain and transport large quantities of money in cash or foreign currencies, and you may need to do this outside of normal banking hours and/or channels. For example, in a 1974 incident in Nicaragua, the Somoza government agreed to pay the Sandinista National Liberation Front a substantial ransom as part of the settlement when the FSLN had taken hostage a number of foreign diplomats and Nicaraguan officials during a raid on a diplomatic reception. In order to raise the funds, they sought the help of the U.S. government and, in the space of a few hours on a Saturday night, the State Department and the Federal Reserve made the necessary arrangements to assist the Nicaraguan government to gain access to funds on deposit in the United States. These funds were then transported to Nicaragua on a special plane and delivered by the Nicaraguan government to the Sandinistas. Within your Crisis Action Team, someone must have this type of expertise, to avoid unnecessary delays. In a kidnapping incident, should your organization elect to pay a ransom, this could be essential to the safe release of the victim.

Should your emergency involve a situation in which the damage and the number of affected people are significant, then it is likely that national or international relief agencies will become involved. It will facilitate matters considerably if your Crisis Action Team includes a relief operations specialist who can maintain liaison with these agencies. This person should understand how these organizations operate, their rules and procedures, and the types of help that can be expected from them. This person can also ensure that any unilateral relief actions initiated by your own organization are coordinated with and complementary to the wider effort.

Most of the emergencies touched upon in this handbook will involve some medical aspect. Additionally, the stress experienced by the Crisis Action Team, families of victims, and others will have a medical component. Your organization's planning should provide for this and the Crisis Action Team should have available to it facilities and expertise in the medical area. In the case of a chemical or industrial accident, for example, the Crisis Action Team should be certain its public pronouncements do not inadvertently contain the type of medical misinformation that could undermine the organization's credibility.

Chapter 8 deals with the trauma emergencies can produce in people. Like public affairs, how an organization is seen to have responded to this facet of the emergency is extremely important. Working and personal relationships can be affected forever. For that reason, we cannot place too much stress on the need for a person on the Crisis Action Team to be charged with the responsibility of assisting victims and their families. *Most people are neither prepared for nor equipped to handle a situation of this type and, therefore, may require special and extraordinary kinds of assistance.*[2] Having the right person performing this function effectively will pay greater dividends than almost anything else the Crisis Action Team does—especially because this task is likely to be performed in the glare of the media.

In any multinational organization, it is most likely that the scene of the emergency will be at some distance from the organization's headquarters (which is where the Crisis Action Team will meet). Therefore, some system of contact with the incident site must be established and someone must be assigned to monitor developments, pass instructions, and request information. Additionally, because there may be another crisis team at the site (or at least a spokesperson), it is essential for the site and headquarters to be in constant contact and to closely coordinate their activities.

Finally, in terms of expected functional requirements for the Crisis Action Team, any organization that operates internationally will want to consider appointing a particular person to handle international contacts. While much of this is being done by others (public affairs with international media, government liaisons, etc.), organizations involved in the staging of major events such as the Olympic Games or trade fairs will find that many international contacts tend to fall between the cracks when they do not fit neatly into other prearranged areas of responsibility. An international generalist on the Crisis Action Team can avoid this problem.

CRISIS MANAGEMENT TEAM DUTIES

As we have noted previously, crises can be divided into three phases: pre-event, event, and postevent. The job of the Crisis Action Team leader is to ensure that the team is involved in and accomplishes a number of discreet tasks in each phase. Only when the crisis management role is seen as a whole that encompasses all three phases can it effectively cope with the crisis itself.

PRE-EVENT

Figure 5–2 depicts the *minimum* duties of the Crisis Action Team during the period before an emergency. In many ways, these are logistical and preparatory

Supervise the Formulation of Policies
Ensure the Development of Procedures
Participate in Preparing Plans
Oversee and Participate in Exercise of Plans
Select Crisis Management Center
Supervise Equipping of Crisis Management Center
Select Crisis Management Center Personnel
Participate in Personnel Training
Review Preparation of Materials
Delegate Authority
Brief Personnel
Ensure the Assembly of Supplies
Ensure Preparation of Rest, Food, Medical Areas

Figure 5–2. Crisis Action Team Duties—before a Crisis

functions, but if they are left until the team is actually dealing with a crisis, then any number of difficulties are inevitable. The Crisis Action Team leader must take the initiative in ensuring that these items are accomplished and maintained.

We discussed earlier the importance of establishing and communicating clear organizational policies well in advance of any possible emergency. The Crisis Action Team must ensure that this is done and must take the lead in suggesting to senior decision-makers what those policies should be. Only *after* these policies are enunciated can procedures be formulated to implement them.

The Team will want to ensure that the procedures are straightforward and sufficient to accomplish their purposes. One example is shown in the flow chart depicted in figure 5–3. This diagram presents one possible system to ensure that the Crisis Action Team is notified of the emergency at the earliest possible moment. It also serves as a reminder to team members of what their initial actions should be. The development of these and other required procedures will ensure the smooth transition by the Crisis Action Team from normal operations to emergency action. In most types of emergencies, the initial hours are among the most critical. If your Crisis Action Team must labor to establish itself instead of concentrating on the emergency, then you may irretrievably prejudice your organization's efforts. Consider, for example, the immediate response to the November 16, 1987 crash of Continental Flight 1713 at Denver's Stapleton International Airport. Despite a serious snowstorm, rescue workers and airport officials were able to react immediately and effectively. It helped, of course, that only a few months previously, the airport had tested its crash plan through a simulation. (See chapter 9 for more on the benefits of simulations.)

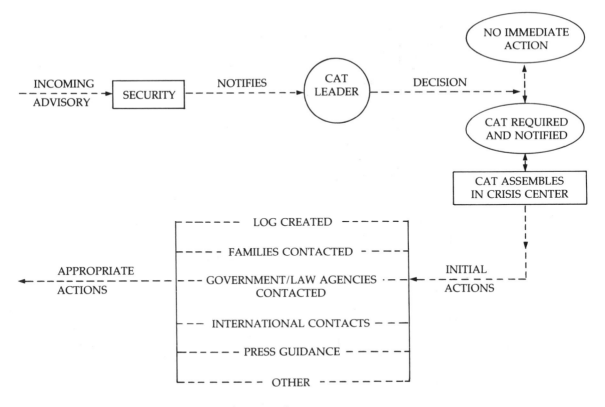

1. Security receives initial report of emergency.
2. Security notifies Crisis Action Team leader.
3. Team leader decides if immediate action is required.
4. If immediate action is required, team leader notifies other team members to convene in Crisis Management Center.
5. Initial liaisons established and actions taken:
   - create log
   - contact family of involved employees
   - make appropriate government/law enforcement liaison contacts
   - prepare contingency press guidance
   - other (contact: offices, unions, etc.)
6. Continuing actions respond to events: media contacts, family liaison, log maintenance, reports.

Figure 5–3. The Chain of Events during a Crisis

The Crisis Action Team as a whole should participate actively in the development of *all* emergency planning. Each member of the team should have been selected because of specific strengths and experiences. In order to ensure complete and effective planning, each team member should participate in planning those sections most relevant to his or her principal tasks(s) during an emergency. Additionally, each team member should be part of the review process for the entire plan. As the plan is tested and updated, each team member should be given the opportunity to provide input on a continuing basis.

Part of this process involves participation in regular exercises of all or part of the emergency plan. In chapter 9, we have set out our views on the importance of simulations as an emergency planning tool. We strongly recommend the regular use of exercises to ensure that your plans work as well in practice as they appear to on paper. This important training tool need not be used elaborately nor need it inordinately disrupt your organization's day-to-day operations. At this point, we merely highlight the importance of ensuring that *all* members of the Crisis Action Team participate in such exercises.

The team will have to function within the physical and equipment limitations of whatever space has been allocated to it. In chapter 6, we provide some suggestions to assist you in identifying the type of Crisis Management Center your organization will require and help you begin the process of selecting and equipping it. For now, remember that the team should be involved and familiar with its capabilities and limitations.

Part of this process includes participation in the selection of equipment for the Crisis Management Center. This does not mean the team must concern itself with brand names and model numbers; rather, team members should set the tone by identifying preferences based on performance requirements and the categories of equipment with which they are comfortable. In this fashion, training requirements can be identified as well. The team—especially the leader— must also monitor the acquisition and installation of the equipment to assure that the center becomes fully operational at the earliest possible moment. The leader should see that the center's equipment is regularly tested and that updating, rotation, and replacement of the equipment takes place as appropriate.

The administrative member of the Team should take the lead in selecting the support personnel who will staff the center. These people must become familiar with the center and with their responsibilities during an emergency. Training and other requirements must be identified and a system established to ensure that these requirements are met.

Each team member should participate in training. This can be done in exercises such as those described in chapter 9 and Appendix D. This can also be done in one-on-one or small group sessions in which one or more team members provide specialized instruction to center personnel. Among the useful byproducts of such sessions is the fostering of interaction between team members and center personnel. Working relations should benefit and emergency action will be made easier, smoother, and more effective. We have found in our own experiences that our ability to effectively and rapidly perform our crisis functions depended heavily upon our having fostered and maintained good working relationships with the people whose assistance and cooperation we would need in case of emergency.

The team will want to be closely involved in preparing materials ranging from statements of work and job descriptions to reviews of training materials. Policy statements and memoranda describing procedures to implement them should be routed through the team leader at a minimum (preferably, the entire team will have the opportunity to review them) prior to their general distribution. Team members should see any studies or reports that affect the organization's emergency preparedness.

Once the team has identified center personnel and established emergency procedures, the team leader (with the assistance of the other members) should carefully delegate authorities to key personnel as appropriate. Just as the team leader requires certain authority along with his or her responsibilities, so do support personnel. Without this delegation of authority, it is unlikely they will act to ease the team leader's burden. The leader will end up dealing with details that should be left to others. In the absence of clear delegation(s) of authority, personnel will be reluctant to act when necessary and they may be unable to implement decisions once they are made.

At this point, the Crisis Action Team should hold regular briefings for center personnel. This will accomplish a number of important things. It will promote the concept of teamwork essential to the smooth running of the team's activities. It will also keep everyone up-to-date on the latest developments and the current thinking and expectations of the Crisis Action Team leader and the organization as a whole. Finally, it will enable the Crisis Management Center's personnel to swing into action at the earliest possible moment of an emergency.

The final two functions in figure 5–2 are primarily the responsibility of the administrative member of the Crisis Action Team, under the oversight of the team leader. The team must have the assurance that required supplies in required quantities are instantly available when needed. Mechanisms to ensure that this occurs at the outset of an emergency are essential, as are mechanisms for their replenishment. Finally, should the emergency be one of duration or require monitoring of events half a world away, facilities must be established to ensure that the Crisis Action Team members and the Crisis Management Center's other personnel can rest, go to the bathroom, eat, and take care of any needed medical requirements. This is an essential part of designing your organization's Crisis Management Center and the team must not overlook it.

Having firmly established the minimum composition of emergency responses and the personnel who will implement them, let us now turn our attention to the core functions of the Crisis Action Team during the event.

EVENT

Figure 5–4 highlights the core functions the Crisis Action Team must expect to fulfill in any emergency.

Once the emergency is upon you, the team leader must determine if the situation is likely to extend beyond the immediate workday. If so (and most emergencies do, especially if they occur well away from headquarters), then he or she should immediately establish shifts and arrange for key personnel to turn over their daily chores to others (optimally, you have provided for this in your planning). It is important to remember that "burnout" is one of the greatest potential dangers crisis management personnel confront. There is always a feeling of wanting to be "where the action is" and of feeling indispensable. The best way to minimize this is to clearly establish at the outset that personnel are only to be working during particular shifts unless otherwise instructed. This holds true for the team leader/alternate as well. It is vital that all personnel be rested, fed, and generally operating at peak efficiency if your crisis is to be successfully managed. This can be a particular problem for civilian government agencies.

The team leader must delegate tasks. We have mentioned the importance of this already and we will repeat it now. The job of the crisis manager is to *manage* and management means setting goals and priorities, selecting the right people to perform tasks and training them, and letting them do their jobs. If you are going to waste (that's right, it is a waste) your time and energy on picking nits,

---

Establish Shift Schedules Immediately
Delegate Tasks—Especially Smaller Ones
Focus on the Underlying Problem, Not the Symptoms
Maintain Control over Workflow, Paper, Etc.
Follow Organizational Policies
Use Your Procedures
Innovate as Needed—Don't be Enslaved by Procedure
Ensure that Information is Shared with the Entire Team
Review *All* Press Releases and Public Statements
Double-check and Confirm Your Information if Possible
Aid Victims and Their Families
Organize/Supervise to Ensure that Work Gets Done
Try to Anticipate
Control Stress for Team Members as Much as Possible
Ensure Log Maintenance

Figure 5–4. Crisis Action Team Duties—during a Crisis

then you are not a manager![3] As a crisis manager, your job is to create the proper environment for the solving of problems associated with your emergency, which brings us to our next point.

You, as a crisis manager, must maintain control over the flow of work, paper, information, and everything else. If not, the Crisis Action Team will quickly become inundated and very little will be accomplished. Now is when procedures swing into action. The executive assistant and the administrative team member will combine to make sure things are done in an orderly manner and that nothing "slips through the cracks."

This will enable the leader to focus on the underlying problems of the emergency and not become distracted by symptomatic concerns. If the small tasks have been properly delegated and the procedures are working properly, the team leader and alternate can attack the crisis itself. This is their most important role because an unidentified crisis cannot be managed. Once you have identified the *real* crisis you can more easily determine appropriate actions and, equally important, what is within your capabilities.[4]

Earlier we noted that the Crisis Action Team should be involved in the development of the organization's policies. This is because they will have to respond to any emergency within the guidelines of those policies. For example, if the organization has a non-negotiation policy in kidnappings or hostage situations, then the Crisis Action Team will proceed differently than if the organization allows negotiation. In a disaster, the organization's policies concerning for whom and to what extent it will provide assistance will determine the team's actions. *If crisis actions and organizational policies disagree, then one or the other **must** be changed to avoid confusion during an emergency.*

For this reason, we stress the importance of having the Crisis Action Team involved in policy-making. If one or more team members have experience in crisis management, the team's input can help assure that the organization's policies are not only reasonable, but workable as well. Once the basic policies are decided, the team leader must see that they are followed in practice, by developing procedures that will be followed automatically during an emergency.

Procedures are like road maps; they help you to establish the most effective way to get where you want to go. To be effective, they must be written down and made available to those who will need to use them. And just as with a map, the user should review emergency procedures in advance of their use. Briefing sessions, exercises, and other training will help to ensure that the team and other emergency personnel are conversant and comfortable with them. Above all, procedures should be flexible and changeable—just like any other facet of your emergency planning. These steps will greatly increase the likelihood that your procedures will be followed. Figure 5–3 is an example of documenting a procedure. The team leader must monitor the team's activities to ensure that the procedures are followed. *If there is a breakdown between the implementation of organizational policies and the use of the emergency procedures, the procedures should be modified to make them usable and in conformance with policies.*

However, the team leader must be alert to the possibility of becoming a slave to procedure. It is one thing to have a viable procedure previously tested and satisfactory. It is quite another thing to have a situation occur for which procedures are either nonexistent or inadequate. Even the best plan may not have foreseen a particular contingency. The team leader must allow for initiative on the part of team members in such situations. Innovation and creativity are often a part of effective crisis management. This is not a license to ignore procedure; rather, it is a recognition of the fact that slavish reliance upon procedure may not always be appropriate.

One of the surest ways to destroy an effective crisis team and undermine the effectiveness of your organization's crisis response is to withhold information from the team. We have seen this far too often. Sometimes, necessary intelligence or information is withheld for "need to know" reasons or to protect sources and methods, etc. If your Crisis Action Team members are to do their jobs, this is foolish. The members of the team should have the proper clearances to receive such information and they should have been selected for their discretion. After all, this is part of their competence to perform in a crisis. The results of withholding information can jeopardize more than working relationships. During a hostage/barricade situation in which one of the authors was closely involved, one part of the U.S. government withheld a key message from another part. This message was crucial to the dispatch of a small team of specialists requested by our ambassador to assist a friendly government in responding to the emergency. The resulting delay slowed the U.S. response by over a day. Fortunately, no lives were lost as a result. *If a Crisis Action Team member cannot receive information relevant to his duties, then he or she does not belong on the team.* By definition, crisis management duties should mean that need-to-know requirements have been resolved for the duration of the emergency.

But the outright withholding of information is only part of the story. We often have seen that a team member who happens to be seated at the far end of the table from the team leader simply does not hear reports being given to the leader. (In fact, during simulations in which we have participated at U.S. Embassies around the world, this is one of the specific things tested.) The team leader should ensure that *all* members are kept abreast of the latest information, developments, and decisions, and that, as new shifts come on duty, these facts are made known to all replacement and/or backup personnel. This can be accomplished by holding periodic briefings for all personnel, by maintaining clipboards with relevant information, or in a variety of other ways. The important thing is that the team leader constantly monitors the situation.

Crisis management is a public affair. Even in situations in which there is a great need for secrecy (for example, in terrorist situations), there will be a large public component. Therefore, as we point out in chapter 7, the public affairs management function is of extreme importance. For this reason, the Crisis Action Team leader must work closely with the public affairs person on the team and *all* public statements and press releases **must** be reviewed by the leader or alternate leader. This will ensure that the most current information and decisions will be accurately reflected in such statements or releases, as well as involving relevant team members in their preparation. Two other important reasons for such within-team review is to ensure that all team members are aware of what is being said publicly in the organization's name and to ensure that any prior notifications (to family members, for example) have been made.

A follow-up to that concerns the importance of double-checking and verifying information received by the Crisis Action Team, if at all possible. Regardless of the source of the information, the team leader should follow the same rule that intelligence agencies and journalists employ: be wary of information unless it has multiple sourcing.[5] Acting precipitously on the basis of incomplete or erroneous information generally will not be in the organization's best interests.

Depending on the type of emergency, a major responsibility of the Crisis Action Team is to ensure that victims and their families receive the type and quantity of assistance required. This aid will be governed by the organization's policies and procedures, but the team must make sure it happens. The team member responsible for liaison with families and other affected persons will be the point person in this regard and will need to keep the team leader current about how this help is progressing and being received. The team should also bear in mind that their own families may need to be provided for, at least for the duration of the emergency. Team members should not be unnecessarily distracted from their crisis duties because their absence from home is creating hardships for their own families. The organization should consider ways and means to relieve team members of some of this burden.

In summary, the team leader/alternate leader must make certain that the Crisis Action Team is organized to ensure that the necessary work gets done in a timely and effective fashion. One of the leader's principal responsibilities will be to supervise (manage, if you will) the team to see that this happens. This is the foundation upon which all crisis management is based. If the leader does not retain control over the team's activities, then the team is likely to lose control over the crisis.

With effective control over the team's activities and with proper supervision and delegation freeing the team leader and alternate from preoccupation with details, it will be possible for them to attempt to anticipate events. The ability to reflect on the course of events and to analyze where things may be heading will enable the team leader(s)—and, therefore, the team itself—to get ahead of the power curve, thereby maximizing opportunities and minimizing dangers and damage to the organization. (One example of this would be when the team leader decides that the time is right to begin recovery operations outlined in the plan although the emergency has not yet ended.)

A principal concern of the Crisis Action Team leader(s) must be to create the best possible environment within which the team can operate. If the pre-event responsibilities have been met and if the Crisis Management Center has been well-equipped, then the important thing at this point is for the team leader to control the stress under which the team functions as much as possible. This can be done in a number of ways.

Proper scheduling of shifts will help mitigate stress by providing major breaks for team members. Team leaders wisely will seek out other opportunities to give team members shorter breaks. But perhaps the most help the team leader(s) can provide in this regard will be to shield team members from outside pressures— that is, from the direct interference of nonteam personnel in the form of supernumeraries and from attempted involvement of nonteam personnel in team activities. A crisis attracts all sorts of unnecessary personnel and advice. The emergency will bring with it a large measure of stress (people's lives may be at stake) and anything the team leader can do to eliminate unnecessary pressures will improve team morale and effectiveness.

Finally, the team leader must ensure that a crisis log is maintained. This will be a principal responsibility of the executive assistant, but the leader will want to review it periodically. There will be temptations during the emergency to overlook this important function, but this can prove disastrous. The log is your record of events as they unfold. It is your way of remembering what was done and what remains to be done. It is also an important element in your ability to reconstruct events later, whether in internal evaluations or in court. Figure 5–5 is an example of what a log might look like. Your log need not be in any particular format nor need it be unnecessarily complicated. The important thing is that it be complete.

Following these guidelines will enable the Crisis Action Team to devote its attention and activities toward the successful management of the crisis. But its job does not stop there. Chapter 10 goes into some detail regarding postemergency return to normalcy. We would like now merely to stress the highlights of postevent duties.

POSTEVENT

Just as the Crisis Action Team must be involved in preparing organizational policies, procedures, and plans, so too must the team actively be involved in

INCIDENT NAME/DESCRIPTION: <u>SAMUELS KIDNAPPING</u>

CAT LEADER/ALTERNATE: <u>V.P. CHARLES SMITH/V.P. JAMES JONES</u>
CAT MEMBERS: _____

DATE: _____
INCIDENT LOG NUMBER: _____ OF _____

DATE/TIME	ACTIVITY DESCRIPTION	COMMENTS
12/XX/XX 0230	CAT CONVENES	
0233	POLICE PHONED	NO ADDITIONAL INFO.: DET. SGT. CURRY IS CONTACT
0238	SAMUELS' WIFE PHONES FOR INFO	PROMISED UPDATE AT 0600
0530	PRESS GUIDANCE #1 RELEASED	
0603	SAMUELS' WIFE UPDATED	
0710	TODAY SHOW NEWS CARRIES STORY	
0723	UPI PHONES	PROMISED CALLBACK

Figure 5–5. Sample Incident Development Log

the evaluation of the effectiveness of these policies, procedures, and plans. The surest test of the effectiveness of these items is the crucible of implementation. Only when the plan is used can the organization learn how useful it is. That is the principal reason why we so strongly advocate the use of simulations during training (see chapter 9). The answers to the basic questions of completeness and effectiveness of your planning can be obtained before a crisis, but as we have said before, even the most complete and effective plan may require revision in the light of its performance in an actual emergency.[6] The plan, after all, is really the embodiment of the organization's decisions on policies and procedures to implement them—either of which may require modification in the wake of experience.

Along with this evaluation of your plan's performance, the Crisis Action Team should evaluate the procedures used during the emergency. (See figure 5–6.) Did they elicit the desired performance from the team and supporting personnel? Did they facilitate or hinder decision-making and implementation? Where they

Evaluate the Effectiveness of Your Plans
Evaluate the Adequacy of Your Procedures
Evaluate the Performance of Your Personnel
Debrief Personnel
Evaluate the Equipment and Training You Used
Revise Your Plans in the Light of New Experience
Revise Procedures
Reward Personnel Appropriately
Arrange an Orderly Transition to Normal Conditions
Assist Victims as Appropriate
Document Events
Prepare After-action Reports Promptly
Retain Archives

Figure 5–6. Crisis Action Team Duties—after a Crisis

properly used? The answers to these and other questions will tell the organization if additional modifications are required.

An important part of the overall evaluation process is a look at how well the people performed. This is not just a cursory glance involving their willingness to work long hours or to be available on short notice. Rather, this is an in-depth examination of the dynamics of the Crisis Action Team and its supporting staff. This involves thoughtful consideration of the personal interactions among team members and other personnel; the facility with which people performed their jobs; the degree of true help individuals provided (it is not inconceivable that an individual may have been more of a hindrance than a help); the amount of additional training that might increase a person's effectiveness; and similar issues. If a mistake was made in assigning a particular task to an individual—or if the person simply does not belong on an emergency team—then now is the time to make adjustments in as face-saving a way as possible.

The personnel effectiveness question is always difficult because of the subjective nature of many of the decisions to be made in this area. For this reason, it is vital that the team leader and any others involved in this phase of the evaluation talk directly to all of the personnel involved in the emergency. Debriefings of crisis personnel *must* be an important part of the evaluation process. Their insights and perspectives will enable a truer picture to be drawn than the subjective recollections and judgments of a few people. Very often the senior people are unaware of the problems encountered by their juniors and have an unrealistic picture of how things went.

We have experienced many situations in which training was denied to crisis management personnel who were nonetheless expected to understand and successfully cope with emergencies. Often, large organizations seem to equate age or seniority with competence. Then, if things do not work out, the individual—not the system—is blamed and the most junior and inexperienced person suffers. Only with proper training and experience can individuals be expected to cope adequately with their responsibilities.

Another important facet of the postincident evaluation is a review of how well the equipment, facilities, and training used to prepare for and respond to the emergency worked. If there were shortcomings, were they a result of a specific problem or were they a systemic dysfunction? Are there repairs that can be easily accomplished, or is a complete overhaul indicated? Were people as prepared as possible for the emergency? Again, negative answers do not necessarily reflect discredit on either individuals or process. *But they might!*

The experience through which your organization has just passed may have been extremely traumatic. It may have resulted from your own acts of omission or commission, or it may have been an act of God. Regardless of the causes of the emergency, surviving it earns your organization the right to objectively examine its methods of operation and its level of preparation. We encourage you to make use of it by examining your plans in light of the experience(s) you have just had and making the appropriate alterations. This may not be easy, given the sensitivities of some to perceived criticism implied by any changes, but it is essential if the organization is to benefit fully from its recent experience(s).[7]

Along with scrutiny of the plan, examination of the procedures (and even the organization's policies) is in order at this stage. As we have previously noted, any inconsistencies between your procedures as they are designed and the way in which they are employed (or not employed) are cause for concern. The team will be in the best position to know how well the existing procedures functioned during the emergency. Making any modifications now will pay great dividends during the next emergency situation.

Even while the Crisis Action Team is evaluating the effectiveness of the existing plans and procedures, the team leader should be considering who among the emergency personnel are deserving of special recognition for their work. At the same time, the organization as a whole should be considering which nonemergency personnel are also deserving of recognition for their efforts in making sure that the organization's daily work was accomplished. As we have previously mentioned, the Crisis Action Team must be free to devote its entire attention to the emergency. Very often, its ability to do so is a direct function of the extraordinary efforts of secretaries, subordinates, and others who are not involved in emergency actions, but are working longer-than-normal hours and performing the jobs of team members. These people, too, deserve recognition. Organizations often are miserly in ways that adversely affect employee morale;

the presentation of attractive certificates, pins, or other mementos is an inexpensive and effective way to organizationally say thank you.

As we will discuss more fully in chapter 10, an important part of the Crisis Action Team's responsibility is to provide for the transition to normality from the emergency. This includes personnel and operational concerns. Everyone involved in the emergency will have been working for some time (often, for a considerable period of time) under great stress and at an emotional high. After all, lives may have depended upon the actions of the Crisis Action Team. The transition to normal operations must recognize and provide for a "decompression" period during which people can rest and mentally readjust to the often humdrum daily routine that constitutes normal activity for the organization. To expect this to occur overnight is unrealistic.

Part of this readjustment may include continuing assistance to victims of the incident. During the emergency, the Crisis Action Team will oversee much of this effort, but once things return to normal, the team is no longer available for such matters. But the continuing commitment of the organization toward those injured while working on its behalf is an important part of the return to normalcy—not only for the victim(s), but for the organization and its employees as a group. The public image of the organization will be affected and other employees will be likely to reassess their own views of the organization in the light of this commitment. Inattention to this facet of crisis management can be costly.

Before disbanding, the Crisis Action Team must document the events surrounding the emergency and the organization's response to it. We have noted previously the importance of having this sort of a record. This process will depend heavily on the accuracy and completeness of your crisis logs and the debriefings of your personnel. This documentation should be prepared as soon after the emergency as is possible. It can be amended later as final details become available. Promptness is especially important to head off any inappropriate recriminations as well as to facilitate the self-review process. And, although this seems self-evident, we stress the importance of retaining this documentation in a readily accessible location for future use. You would be surprised at how often the wheel is reinvented for emergency action because no records of previous plans or emergency actions can be found. (On second thought, we are sure that many of you know this from your own experiences.) Often, the records do not exist, and, more often, they simply cannot be found—which is another way of saying the same thing. Don't let this happen to you.[8]

But even the best-prepared and most effective Crisis Action Team cannot be successful if it must labor under inadequate circumstances. For that reason, let's turn now to some considerations relevant to your Crisis Management Center.

EVALUATING YOUR PLAN AFTER A CRISIS: A CHECKLIST

✔ Evaluate how useful the plan was.

✔ Identify any problems revealed during the incident.

✔ Determine if the plan's procedures were followed and if they were effective. If not, examine ways to improve them.

✔ Determine how quickly the Crisis Action Team was able to organize and begin to function.

✔ Determine the adequacy of the facilities and resources provided to the Crisis Action Team. Consider how can they be improved.

✔ Determine if information was shared effectively and fully within the Crisis Action Team and identify any reasons for a negative answer.

✔ Determine if the team members and support personnel were familiar with the organization's operating procedures and chain of command.

✔ Determine if your organization's personnel were familiar with the procedures of other involved organizations.

✔ Examine the effectiveness of your organization's liaison(s) with external actors such as government officials, families, and the media.

✔ Determine if routine matters were referred to appropriate personnel or whether the Crisis Action Team allowed itself to be distracted by them.

✔ Review your reports and statements to determine if information was reported accurately, on a timely basis, and in the proper fashion. Determine if appropriate analyses were prepared as required. Check that the proper people and organizations were kept informed.

✔ Determine whether your supplies were adequate.

✔ Review the effectiveness of your public affairs management.

✔ Determine the effectiveness of your rumor control mechanism.

✔ Examine the composition of your crisis action team to determine if personality factors impeded effective crisis management.

✔ Review the involvement of your Crisis Action Team in the planning and preparation of your emergency procedures to determine its adequacy and effectiveness.

✔ Review the composition of your Crisis Action Team to determine its adequacy.

✔ Review the training of your emergency personnel to determine its effectiveness, completeness and adequacy.

THE CRISIS MANAGEMENT CENTER: LOCATION AND LAYOUT

6

On 1 October 1987 a 5.9-level earthquake gave California State University at Los Angeles the opportunity to see how well its recently completed earthquake-response plan worked. The twenty-two-thousand-student school was successfully evacuated (although one student died when a parking structure collapsed) despite the considerable damage sustained by the university.

CalState LA had made good use of a special operations center it established and equipped with everything from telephones to supplies for the emergency personnel. According to the university's police chief, "there would have been a great deal of disarray" in the absence of the plan.

Despite this and other examples of successful preparation, a number of California officials remain concerned about the state's ability to survive the truly massive earthquake (above level 8 on the Richter scale), which has been predicted to occur. A study by the Federal Emergency Management Agency says that such an earthquake would be the greatest domestic disaster since the Civil War. Efforts by state and local governments to enhance preparations for such a quake have been increased in the wake of the October 1 experience.[1]

It is not enough for an organization to formulate its policies, select its Crisis Action Team, and create emergency plans and operating procedures. The questions of *where* the Crisis Action Team will perform its function and the types and quantities of its equipment must be addressed. As we have written elsewhere:

The physical location and equipping of the Crisis Management Center are considerations which are too often overlooked until an incident occurs. At that time, the Crisis Action Team is forced to utilize whatever available space is at hand. Careful forethought will enable the company to have available an area either previously equipped—or capable of ·rapidly being equipped—to respond to any contingency.[2]

Picking your spot for crisis management should occur coincidentally with the other preparations identified throughout this book, not at the last minute.

Crisis Management Centers can range from the dedicated twenty-four-hour operations centers maintained by many government agencies to little more than a spare office or conference room used *ad hoc* as circumstances require. We have worked in all kinds of dedicated and *ad hoc* facilities. The latter type of arrangement is the most common. There is no mandate that your organization have any particular type of Crisis Management Center. What is important is that you identify your needs and create the type of Crisis Management Center best suited to your own requirements.

Elsewhere in this book, there are photographs of several of the well-equipped and staffed operations centers of some U.S. government organizations, along with some of a mobile center used by one Fortune 500 corporation (which wishes to remain unidentified). These represent the range of options available to any organization. Figure 6–1 depicts a possible configuration for a Crisis Management Center that a small- to medium-sized corporation may wish to employ.

The location of your Crisis Management Center should be as close as possible to the normal workplaces of your organization's senior management. However, you will not want the activities of the center to interfere with the normal work of your organization, which must also be done during the emergency. In addition, the center should not attract the attention of visitors to your headquarters. The specific location of your Crisis Management Center will be determined in most cases by what spare space might be available, by the size of the Crisis Action Team, and by the amount of equipment the team expects to use in an emergency. Equally important, the center must incorporate or be close to sleeping, medical, food, sanitation, and relaxation facilities. You must also consider whether you should have an alternative (or backup) center and your need for some type of center at the scene of the emergency.

A government agency might require a dedicated facility for crisis management, but most private sector organizations should probably consider using a conven-

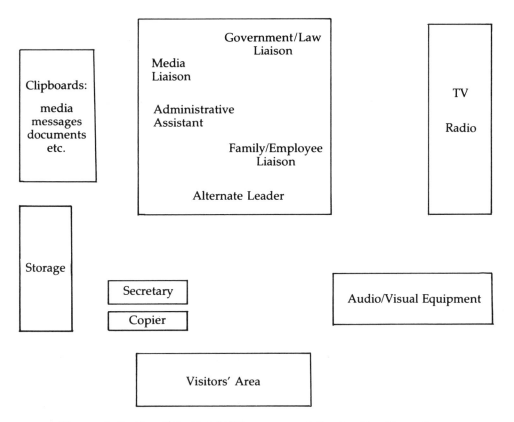

Figure 6–1. Possible Crisis Management Center Configuration

ient conference room in the suite of the president of the corporation. Regardless of your decision, there are certain requirements essential for a functioning Crisis Management Center. These fall into several basic categories: power, communications, information, operational support, and crowd control. We would like to examine each of these in turn to demonstrate how the most fundamental requirements in each category can be met simply and effectively.

POWER

Electricity is essential for the operation of modern equipment ranging from typewriters and computers to telephones and televisions. Without it, the Crisis Action Team's activities will probably come to a halt. If you have determined that your organization requires a dedicated crisis management facility, then your design of that facility will incorporate the necessary electrical amperage and outlets for the equipment you select. However, if your Crisis Action Team will make use of a conference room, office, or some other location that will be pressed into service when needed, then someone must survey the location to ensure that it will be able to function as required.

Most rooms in commercial buildings have at least one electrical outlet, probably a three-wire one. This will not be sufficient for emergency operations. Install baseboard outlets along all walls of the room, or store heavy-duty extension cords in a cabinet or in a drop ceiling—assuming that the use of extension cords presents no fire hazards and that the use of extraordinarily large amounts of electricity in the Crisis Management Center can be supported by the available power supply.

In many cases, insufficient power and/or redundancy will exist. This can be solved by running additional high voltage lines into the center or by using backup power generators.

COMMUNICATIONS

The basic communications tool will be the telephone. Team members will need to talk to other employees, to the site of the emergency, to the media, to family members of victims, and countless others. We recommend that there be at least one telephone line per team member, with several extra lines to permit calls to be held when necessary. If possible, all lines should be routed around the organization's central switchboard to limit the abillity of outsiders to listen in on conversations. If this is not possible, at least one such line should be established for the team's use in conducting especially sensitive conversations.

There are a number of options that should be considered to make the use of telephones more comfortable and efficient. Among them are headsets, speakers, and muting devices. Also useful, where permitted by local telephone companies, are integrated recording equipment and devices which allow a line to be kept open after the other party has hung up (this will permit the tracing of calls when desired).

Organizations should also consider the desirability of telex and telegram addresses and equipment, as well as facsimile capabilities and even two-way radios. Even an organization that already employs one or more of these should determine if additional capabilities are required for crises.

INFORMATION

The most pressing need of your Crisis Action Team during the emergency will be information, timely and in large quantities. The use of telephones and other communications equipment will help provide much information; however, any major emergency will have a large public dimension. The media will be reporting on a continuous basis, statements will be made, commentary might ensue. For this reason, your Crisis Management Center must be equipped adequately with audio and visual equipment such as televisions and radios (both conventional and shortwave). You may wish to consider the use of special TVs that incorporate multiple screens, each of which may be tuned to a different station. In situations in which the media is in competition to see who can outdo whom, this provides you with an efficient way to constantly monitor the airwaves. Special adaptors for conventional TVs are available which, to a limited extent, accomplish this. An additional benefit of this equipment is its use during quiet periods for the relaxation of the Crisis Action Team.

It is important to remember that emergencies resulting from induced catastrophes will often be accompanied by demands made by the perpetrators of the incident. This is especially true in terrorist acts such as kidnappings, hostage-takings, hijackings, or bombings, but many criminal actions also fall into this category. Therefore, if your threat assessment envisions the possibility of such emergencies, you will want to consider having some or all of the following equipment available: a video recorder/player; cassette and reel-to-reel player/recorders; a slide projector and screen; an overhead projector; and even a movie projector. Any or all of these could prove essential during a crisis and you may not be able to afford the delay required to acquire such equipment.

OPERATIONAL SUPPORT

No matter how competent your Crisis Action Team, no matter how well-equipped your Crisis Management Center, if the supporting cast is inadequate, things will go poorly. In crisis management, this supporting cast consists of people and logistics. We suggest you begin your consideration of this matter by developing a floorplan of the Crisis Management Center. This floorplan should identify the placement of equipment and the location of personnel to ensure that everything and everyone is properly located from the beginning of the emergency. Especially important in this regard is the proper identification of telephone lines and secretarial equipment.

The next matter to be evaluated is the type and quantity of office supplies and equipment that will be required. Such things as typewriters, word processors, photocopiers, and their supplies are obvious, but don't forget to consider the need for paper and pencils and such mundane but essential items such as paper clips, clipboards, and staplers. (The obvious is often overlooked in the effort to touch all bases. As Benjamin Franklin wrote in *Poor Richard's Almanac*, ''A little neglect may breed mischief: for want of a nail the shoe was lost; for want of a shoe the horse was lost; for want of a horse the rider was lost.'') Many government agencies and large corporations have developed specialized forms for such things as cables, memoranda, etc.; be certain you have a sufficient supply of the proper forms.

Having assured yourself that you have the proper type and amount of supplies available, turn your attention to storing these items. Most organizations will not have dedicated crisis management facilities. In fact, most organizations will be dealing with emergencies using a convenient office or meeting room, a location used for other things until an emergency occurs. Therefore, the question of storing these items assumes additional importance. The two possible approaches are to have the supplies and equipment stored elsewhere—which in many ways may be like not having assembled it in the first place—or acquiring aesthetic storage cabinets that can be left in the center during nonemergency periods. We strongly recommend the latter approach. Beyond this, we recommend that you develop an inventory of supplies and label them for quick retrieval.

Additionally, part of your emergency planning should include the physical conditions and medicinal requirements of your emergency personnel. This information must be reviewed regularly to ensure that a small supply of required medicines is available during an emergency, in addition to aspirin, antacids, and other common over-the-counter medicaments. These items can be secured in the same storage cabinets as your office supplies. Remember to rotate these medicines as appropriate.

Finally, as we have mentioned elsewhere, it is important that your Crisis Management Center assist the Crisis Action Team to "pace" itself by providing ready access to rest, food, and sanitation supplies. The need for such facilities has been dealt with in other sections of this book, so we will confine ourselves here to merely recommending yet again that you carefully consider this matter.

CROWD CONTROL

However large and well-equipped your Crisis Management Center is, it *will* have a limit to the number of people who can be comfortably accommodated. Certainly, you will want to ensure that your Crisis Action Team is suitably equipped to carry out its functions, but what about the inevitable supernumeraries who will descend upon the center? Every organization will have people who legitimately need to visit periodically for briefings or other reasons, and there will also be those who believe that their status merits (or will be enhanced by) frequent visits to the center. Whether you like it or not, this is a reality of crisis management and you must be prepared to deal with it in ways that do not add to the burdens of your Crisis Action Team.

Over the years, we have been involved in many crises—both real and simulated. We have discovered that necessary visitors to the Crisis Management Center will wish to keep their visits short, while unnecessary ones will often leave once they have been seen there. We recommend that you take advantage of this by having an area set aside for all visitors you cannot keep out of the center, where they can read messages, memoranda, press statements, and so on and sit *un-*comfortably and out of the way of the Crisis Action Team. Some extra chairs and tables supplied with clipboards and other nonsensitive materials will accomplish this. Your organization's internal pecking order may force you to tolerate such intrusions, but you should not allow them to interfere with the important work being done.

If your organization's physical plant permits it, try to incorporate within your Crisis Management Center some additional space that can be used for small group discussions and/or briefings. This will allow the leadership of the Crisis Action Team to leave the main area occasionally for reflection or sensitive discussions.

Finally, in chapter 7, we discuss the importance of having an identified location where the media can expect to receive information and briefings. It should be obvious that this location *cannot* be within or even near the Crisis Management Center if you are to avoid disruptions to the Crisis Action Team's efforts and prevent information leaks. Your efforts to deal with the media and to confine them to one location will be enhanced if you carefully consider the logistical support that reporters will also require to do their jobs. If you can provide this, they are more likely to work within the parameters you establish. If not, read on.

THE CRISIS MANAGEMENT CENTER: A CHECKLIST

- ✔ Determine the type of Crisis Management Center best suited to your organization's requirements.

- ✔ Identify the location and the required equipment for your Crisis Management Center.

- ✔ Consider how to balance the aesthetic and operational requirements of your Crisis Management Center, especially if the location will be used for other purposes during normal operations.

- ✔ Ensure that your Crisis Management Center is operational by regularly checking all supplies, equipment, and facilities in place.

✔ Establish a program of regular checks of supplies and equipment to ensure that they are regularly rotated to maintain freshness, as appropriate, and to keep them operational.

✔ Ensure that your Crisis Management Center has provisions for necessary power, personnel, and facilities (such as sanitation, rest, food, etc.).

✔ Identify your communications requirements and ensure that they are satisified.

✔ Consider the need for any upgrades required for your Crisis Management Center and ensure that they are accomplished.

✔ Establish access control procedures for the Crisis Management Center, keeping in mind the likelihood that visitors or other noncrisis team personnel may need to be accommodated.

CRISIS COMMUNICATIONS

7

When families of the victims of Northwest Flight 255 arrived in Detroit after the August 16, 1987 crash which killed all on board except a four-year-old girl, the airline was prepared to provide for their every need. Some observers praised the airline's handling of the catastrophe, others accused the airline of seeking merely to reduce its ultimate payout to families. Northwest's vice-president for public relations assured the world that "our people were there out of a sense of caring and commitment. . . . Some of our people became totally involved, almost part of the family."[a]

However, the company did not fare so well in the immediate aftermath of the crash. In the hours after the crash, while firefighters and rescue workers struggled to deal with the situation, a volunteer firefighter discovered the young girl, still alive, in the sheltering arms of her dead mother. His perception and quick action saved her life. Coincidentally, he was a maintenance worker employed by Northwest. However, it was learned the next day that because he had not reported for work cleaning airplanes that evening, he was to be docked a day's pay. Undoubt-

---

[a]*Washington Post*, August 27, 1987.

edly this decision was later reversed, but, if so, it has been lost in the shuffle. What should have been a public relations triumph for Northwest turned into a black eye.

One of the cornerstones of American democracy is a free press, a right so fundamental that it was written into the very first amendment to the Constitution in the earliest days of the Republic. The Fourth Estate has by and large performed its role very creditably over the last two hundred years or so, and it has been in no small part responsible for the preservation of those freedoms we hold dear. But the very nature of a free press carries with it certain inherent difficulties. Besides its role as guardian of liberty, the press is also, very simply, a business. The pressures of the marketplace operate on ideas and information as surely as they apply to goods and services. If people don't buy your product, for whatever reason, you are out of business. If the public doesn't buy your newspaper, or watch the news on your station, or read your magazine, then you won't be in the news-dissemination business for very much longer. For the media, readers and viewers (or listeners) mean advertisers, and advertisers mean revenue, and revenue is the difference between survival and bankruptcy. If you doubt this, just remember that advertisers paid $550,000 for thirty seconds of air time during the 1987 Superbowl and $645,000 for the same time during the 1988 Superbowl. This price can be commanded by TV networks because somewhere in the vicinity of 120 million people were watching.

THE MEDIA ARE ANOTHER TYPE OF BUSINESS

This brings us to the very nature of the news business. News, by definition, is something unusual, something more-or-less sensational. If a thousand airplanes take off and land safely day after day, only passengers and airline personnel are likely to be interested. What would have seemed stupefying or wonderful only fifty years ago is today merely routine—and to most people rather boring. No one is going to pay good money, or spend the time, to read a story about a plane landing safely. But a crash or a near collision, now *that* is another matter.

It is not overly flattering to reflect that most of us would rather read about a plane that crashed than about one that didn't, but that, as we said, is the nature of news. First, because the unusual is inherently interesting and the commonplace is not. And secondly, because violence and destruction seem to be newsworthy for their own sakes. From the point of view of the media (and leaving all obvious moral judgements aside) a plane crash is probably a lot better than a mere near collision. There will be scenes of devastation, pictures of bereaved relatives, interviews with horrified survivors, and so on. Most of all, if there is an issue of human or corporate culpability, you can be sure the media will be trying to find it. And this is one of the most important and visible challenges for a Crisis Action Team.

Any incident of significance and duration is virtually certain to draw media attention, regardless of where it occurs. Hurricanes, fires, riots, meltdowns, acts of terrorism, and acts of God all are sufficiently unusual and sufficiently sensational to be considered newsworthy. Even among such incidents, there is a hierarchy. Only one person died during the TWA 847 hijacking in June 1985, yet Tom Brokaw and Dan Rather were rushed to the scene in Beirut. Conversely, the October 1987 earthquake in California, in which many people died, did not receive such high-level treatment. Apparently, earthquakes in California are inherently less dramatic than hijackings abroad.

Most of us feel a certain ambivalence about the media; we like to see our names in the paper, but we would rather not be bothered with a lot of prying and impertinent questions in the middle of a crisis. Unfortunately, it is pretty much *only* during a crisis that we get that kind of media attention. Since the problem cannot be wished away (would that it could!), it is vital that you anticipate the problem and be prepared to deal with it on your terms. Handled properly, a lot of ultimate good can come out of a crisis situation in terms of good will and public relations. (Remember, crises are composed of both dangers and opportunities.) Handled poorly, the results can haunt you and your organization for many years.

The press, remember, does not have to be your enemy, but its interests are decidedly at variance with your own. Media people are trying to sell newspapers and air time, and this means that they want to be able to offer the public the fullest information, the most sensational aspects, and the goriest details. We mean by this, incidentally, no criticism (not even implied) of the media; they have their job to do and you have yours. Just keep it firmly in mind at all times that these two jobs are quite different. The problem facing the Crisis Action Team member charged with handling public affairs is how to avoid antagonizing reporters without saying anything that may adversely affect an ongoing incident or lead to negative publicity for the organization later on. The purpose of this chapter is to help you plan for, and respond to, this challenge. Our comments are born of years of experience in dealing with the media in varying capacities— both as government employees and as independent experts.

THE "NO COMMENT" TRAP

One obvious way to try to handle the media, and one which has a certain superficial appeal, is an unbroken "no comment." This is not completely a bad approach, since it has the advantage of not risking mistakes or giving away too much information. It won't make you too many friends among reporters trying desperately to get at least some kind of story before their next deadline, but it at least won't give away the store either. The problems with this approach are threefold. First, if reporters can't get anything at all from the designated public affairs officer, some will try every other potential source, regardless of how well or badly informed. Secondly, a refusal to talk at all alienates most people (including the public at large) and gives the impression that you have something to hide. Lastly, a capable reporter can frame a question and/or report your answer in such a way that a "no comment" can be very damaging. In short, you lose the public affairs initiative and all control over this aspect of the crisis.

As to the first problem, it is one that occurs in practically every incident. Most men and women of the media are people of real integrity, who are not out to undermine or damage your operation. But they have a job to do. This means they are going to try to get as much information as possible, as rapidly as possible (remember those deadlines), and from whomever possible. If the designated spokesperson does not give them enough for a story, they will try to find someone who can. If what they learn can't be verified, they may still report it as rumor. Not every newspaper or radio or television station would do that, of course, but you can be sure that some will. And once a rumor is reported, other, more-responsible journalists may feel obligated to mention it also. *Remember, it is always best if the information comes from you!*

In the late 1970s, Hooker Chemical Corporation, a subsidiary of Occidental Petroleum, was savaged by the media for causing—and trying to cover up the results of—massive toxic chemical dumping at Love Canal in New York. Because the company waited years before providing its side of the story to the media, the only information available to the public was from panicked people living in the area and from sensational articles and books written by journalists who accepted the picture of a heartless and environmentally unconcerned corporate giant. By the time Hooker presented its story (which accurately demonstrated that the state of New York was actually to blame for Love Canal's situation), Occidental's stock had lost $500 million in value.

As we said before, most of us find the prospect of seeing our names in the paper very attractive. An employee—even another member of the Crisis Action Team—might be caught unawares, or flattered by the attention, or have his own particular axe to grind. The reasons why someone other than the spokesperson may give information to the media probably cover the entire gamut of human frailties, but the consequences are generally the same: rarely helpful and potentially ruinous.

For this reason, there should be only one spokesperson. He or she should be the only one to talk with representatives of the media. It should be well established in advance—and understood not only by all members of the Crisis Action Team, but by all employees and associates as well (including family members)—that press inquiries of any type concerning an ongoing incident *must* be referred to the designated spokesperson. We stress the application of this principle to inquiries of *any* type. The most seemingly innocent question may carry with it hidden dangers, and nothing is more damaging than to have contradictory information given out, even on relatively minor points.

The only exception to this will be if it becomes necessary to assign someone to handle the media at the scene of an incident. This is sometimes the case with fires and other disasters, as well as with some induced catastrophes such as terrorist acts, when some reporters will be poking around the scene of the event while others are calling the main office. If the two sites are in different cities, or possibly even in different countries, more than one spokesperson probably will be necessary. In such a case, there should be no more than two individuals designated to answer the media's questions—one in the Crisis Management Center and one at the scene.

Under such circumstances, it is crucial that these two coordinate regularly. Ideally, they should clear all statements and briefings with each other in advance. Admittedly, this can be quite difficult if the two sites are well removed from each other, especially in the midst of a crisis, but it is up to the spokespersons to do as much as they can: work out a common approach beforehand; stay in as close contact as is possible; and refer any difficult inquiries for checking with a promise to provide an answer later. The spokesperson in the Crisis Management Center should also clear all statements and briefings with the team leader in advance.

Even if no one other than the appropriate official does talk with the media, there are still problems with an unvarying "no comment" response. The publicity that flows from the kinds of incidents we are discussing can be helpful or hurtful. Long after the emergency situation has faded from memory, you will still have to rely on the good will and high opinion of the public—and your own staff, who will also be forming opinions based on media reporting. This is true to a greater or lesser extent for everyone, but it applies especially to organizations operating in the private sector. Remember the Northwest Airlines incident at the beginning of this chapter. We are not suggesting that journalists are especially vindictive, that they will consciously seek to punish unresponsiveness. But the wrong impression planted in the journalistic mind can have unforseen and undesired consequences long after the fact. After all, reporters are human, too.

More than that, an adamant "no comment" position can give the appearance that you have something to hide. We hasten to point out that you may very well have something to hide, and very good reasons for hiding it. Police departments and government agencies may wish to hold things back for procedural or security reasons, and some things are in fact illegal to divulge. Private companies may have information they do not want made public for proprietary or other reasons that are no less compelling. What we are suggesting you avoid, as far as you can, is the *appearance* of hiding something. A good press statement should reveal as much as possible in order to allow you to protect truly sensitive things from public scrutiny.

Remember that it is the reporters' job to get as full a story as they can, and that their judgment as to the appropriateness of disclosure may be quite different from yours. These are the things of which newspapers' circulations and reporters' promotions are made (not to mention Pulitzer Prizes). Unfortunately, the damage in terms of a specific incident can be tremendous. A classic example occurred a few years ago during a hostage situation: the captor and his victim were in a building surrounded by police. A reporter asked the officer in charge about his plans. The officer remarked that there was another way into the building that would allow his men to surprise the captor. This plan was duly reported to the listening public via the magic of radio. Unfortunately, the man inside the building also had a radio, and the plan was foiled, resulting in the prolongation of the incident and greater danger for everyone concerned.[1] This is an extreme example, but it is not an isolated one and it gives you an idea of the problems which can result.

Nonetheless, the appearance of having something to hide can result in negative publicity. And it can be made to look a great deal worse if the questions carry unspoken implications. We mentioned earlier that questions can be framed in such a way as to make "no comment" an answer in itself, and usually not a very good one. Consider, for example, a situation in which there has been a terrorist attack or a riot. A reporter asks, "Were you prepared for such an attack?" A refusal to respond clearly implies that you were not. "Do you think you have paid sufficient attention to your security needs and the safety of your employees?" "No comment" suggests that you do not think so, and that you don't like being asked the question. It isn't particularly fair, but that's the way it will look.

For all these reasons, you are not likely to be able to get away with a simple refusal to tell the press anything. In view of that, we suggest that you be guided by a few fundamental principles. Individual circumstances will vary, of course, but in general we think that consideration of the following points will save you a few headaches.

DIFFERENCES AMONG THE MEDIA

An important but frequently overlooked facet of media relations is that there are some basic differences among the various media that influence how they cover events and report the news. Of course, there are the liberal–independent–conservative differences, but we refer here to the basic differences between print and electronic media and the styles of reporting of the major U.S. television networks.

PRINT VERSUS ELECTRONIC

The electronic media are much more time-sensitive and immediate in their orientation than are the print media. In practice, this means tighter and more-frequent deadlines—especially for all-news stations. The electronic media will be interested in spot reporting and continuing updates to a greater extent than the print media, which can afford to wait longer before preparing their stories. The type of story carried by TV and radio is more likely to rely on speculation and rumor because there is less time to verify or evaluate information. Previous errors in reporting may never be acknowledged or corrected or they may be rectified so subtly as to escape notice.

Print media, on the other hand, while subject to many of the same pressures as their electronic counterparts, are not in true competition with TV and radio in terms of speed. Rather, they will seek exclusive stories and in-depth analyses, which can distinguish their reporting from that of the electronic media. This is especially true of publications appearing weekly or less frequently. While the print media may seek to downplay their own errors or omissions, because they deal in the written, as opposed to the spoken word, they generally do make corrections in print even if these are buried on an inner page.

The implications of dealing with these differing foci are obvious and do not bear enumerating. They must, however, be kept in mind by the public affairs officer.

STYLISTIC DISTINCTIONS

While the tone and style of the print media are frequently more a function of the ideological persuasion of their ownership, we are all familiar with sensational publications. This stylistic range is more subtle in the electronic media, but it is nonetheless present—especially in the major television networks.

Among the Big Three of American TV, at least one study has detected differences in emphasis and sources for the coverage of disasters and induced catastrophes.[2] The study found that CBS tends to rely on official sources and its coverage seems intended to emphasize the manageability of the crisis. ABC concentrates on ordinary people and stresses the hardships of the event on the affected persons, along with the unmanagability of the crisis. NBC's coverage appears to accept crises as an inevitable fact of life, emphasizing that the particular event will pass and things will return to normal.

Although not included in the study, the growth of the Cable News Network (CNN) into a major rival of the Big Three is a phenomenon that must also be kept in mind. Because CNN is a twenty-four-hour news network, its appetite for information is insatiable and, we believe, it is constantly on the alert for sensational pieces to keep its viewers interested.

While too much can be made of these stylistic distinctions, public affairs spokespeople might profitably tuck these insights away for future reference.

DESIGNATION OF A PUBLIC AFFAIRS OFFICER

It probably goes without saying (but we'll risk saying it anyway) that whoever is going to be dealing with the press should have some experience with the business of public affairs. This may not always be possible, but it is certainly always desirable. A single slip, a piece of incorrect information, a moment of unreflected speculation, can sometimes do a great deal of damage. Your spokesperson should be articulate, well-informed and personable; if he or she has knowledge of the operations of the working press and/or contacts among them, that is all to the good. *It is important to look like you know what you are doing, even if you are still trying to figure it out!*

Your spokesperson should also be a member in good standing of the Crisis Action Team. When decisions are made, or when information is required, immediate and continuous contact will likely be necessary between the public affairs officer and the leader of the team. Good working relations between the two are essential, as they will have to coordinate closely throughout the management of a crisis. This should be taken into account, incidentally, not only in the selection of the spokesperson, but in the selection of the rest of the team as well.

Bear in mind that the needs of public afairs management are different from—and sometimes at odds with—the needs of overall crisis management. We have emphasized the importance of having a single spokesperson, but believe us, it can get pretty lonely out there all by yourself. As the only point of contact with the media, the designated individual must handle all the inquiries, from all the newspapers and radio and TV stations that are interested, on all aspects of the situation. Everyone wants information, and that is usually the thing in shortest supply. The spokesperson will feel that he or she has to tell reporters *something*, if only because he or she is tired of looking like an idiot. The team leader will have other things on his or her mind, and may not be anxious to share them with the press. It is important that these two officials be sensitive to each other's needs and points of view.

At this point, a cautionary note. We have discussed elsewhere the importance of good communications between the Crisis Action Team and victims, employees, families, and other non-media affected persons. We would like to stress that this is *not* the function of the public affairs officer. He or she will be completely occupied with the media. Although the rumor control and affected persons liaison personnel will need to consult the public affairs officer, combining these functions in one person is a prescription for problems.

ANTICIPATION

As we have emphasized throughout this handbook, anticipation is the key to good crisis management. The more that can be discussed and decided upon before the onset of an emergency, the easier everyone's job will be once a crisis materializes. A spokesperson, in consultation with the rest of the team, and subject to the approval of the team leader, should try to anticipate the kinds of questions that will be asked and prepare guidelines for answering them. Some of this can be done in the abstract: "What is your policy toward paying ransom?" "How many employees do you have working in (the location where the emergency has occurred)?" Other answers can be considered only in the light of a specific situation; you can't know that you might be asked about the details of a fire or a hurricane until one actually happens in a specific location. *But under no circumstances should a public affairs officer meet the press unprepared!* Many government agencies have a precise, institutionalized precedure for preparing their public affairs officer. On a daily basis, information is gathered from each organizational component, studied, rewritten, and analyzed in the light of the kinds of questions that are expected. The spokesperson then makes certain that he or she is completely conversant with all the details related to those issues before *any* contact with the media. This ensures that *all* information given to the media reflects the collective expertise of the entire organization. There are enough pitfalls in this business already. Anticipating the questions likely to come up, and the best way to answer them, is an effort that will repay itself many times over. As far as possible, these issues should be discussed, and the decisions made, before the questions are even asked.

SIGNIFICANCE OF STATEMENTS

During a crisis, statements that normally would be routine and unimportant may assume a new significance. We have already discussed the possible interpretations that can be put on a simple "no comment." Unfounded speculation is, of course, to be avoided. You may think privately that an incident may be related to a similar one which took place elsewhere a few weeks earlier, or that a fire might be the result of arson, or that the government of a foreign country might be behind a riot in that country, but we urge you to keep such thoughts to yourself. The press will engage in enough speculation for all of us; your job is to scotch rumors, not to start them.

Remember that even the most cautious answer may lend itself to unwanted press speculation. Suppose, for example, there has been a fire or an explosion. Arson or sabotage is, of course, a much juicier, and therefore more newsworthy, possibility than faulty wiring, so the question is immediately asked, "Do you or your superiors suspect arson/sabotage?" The only reasonable answer in the absence of any evidence one way or the other is something along the lines of

"We will have to wait until an investigation has been conducted." (Notice, by the way, that this is one of those situations where a "no comment" can come across sounding like a "yes.") This is a perfectly legitimate response, but don't be surprised if the resulting story has a headline like, "Spokesman Refuses to Rule Out Arson."

An even more difficult situation arises for police or government officials during a hostage-taking incident. The question is usually asked, sooner or later, "Are you going to rush the building?" or "Are you planning military/police action?" or whatever happens to be appropriate for the occasion relative to the use of force. Now, crisis management, by its very nature, requires that you keep open as many options as possible. Even if you don't plan to use force, there is no reason to let terrorists or criminals know that. The very existence of the possible use of force is a factor in the authorities' favor. Nonetheless, you may not wish to share your thinking with the world at large. (This is especially true if any sort of military/police action is being countenanced.) But a response refusing to rule out the use of force can lead to a headline like "Attack Being Considered," opening the floodgates for all sorts of problems down the line.

To a certain degree, this kind of thing is unavoidable, and is dependent largely on the integrity of the journalist who asks the questions (and the editor behind him or her). Fortunately, most members of the press are responsible professionals; they will try to extract the most publishable story they can—along with the juiciest details—but most will not deliberately do anything to embarrass you. If you try to be as responsive to their needs as the circumstances will allow, respect their deadlines as far as possible, and *anticipate* questions as much as you can, you will save yourself and the people for whom you work a considerable amount of aggravation.

PUBLIC AFFAIRS MANAGEMENT

Having said you should try to frame your position(s) beforehand, a few words are in order as to just what you might say. Obviously, specific responses will depend on the nature of the crisis; whether you are representing a public or private agency; the location, intensity, and duration of the incident; and so forth. In general, though, there are a few important principles to keep in mind.

Before a crisis, emphasis is usually a good thing. There are some situations in which you will have a fair amount of warning, or at least indication, of potential trouble. Hurricanes, for example, have a fairly well-defined season and can almost always be predicted in advance. That is, their existence and possible travel path will be reported, giving everyone who might be in the way some advance warning. Increased airline hijackings, terrorist threats, bomb threats, and heightened anti-American rhetoric all offer a certain amount of warning. The same goes for deteriorating political circumstances in countries in which you have interests. In short, many different types of emergencies do not burst on the scene unexpectedly.

Clearly, your job here is twofold. First, you want to heighten the sensitivities of potential victims, making them aware that a hurricane *is* coming or that they *could* be among the victims of a terrorist attack. Second, you need to disseminate as widely as possible the proper procedures for dealing with the anticipated danger. Hurricanes and terrorist threats being what they are, you may find yourself the subject of considerable media interest. And this is definitely a situation in which the press is on your side. Not only do news stories help to circulate the information you are trying to put out, but they also help to legitimize the seriousness of the threat. (Don't underestimate the importance of this. It can be very difficult to convince people that a threat is real. Most people simply do not want to believe that such a thing could happen to them, or at least don't want to have to deal with the implications of that reality. In much the same way, many people don't draw up wills because it would force them to admit that they expect some day to die.) The media can help you emphasize the nature of the threat and to impress upon your audience the need to take precautions.[3] Use them.

During a crisis, it is generally best to play things down. In the case of a fire or disaster, you normally will want to allay people's fears and to calm things down. A certain number of affected parties will always tend to respond to a crisis in a panicky or emotional manner, usually to the detriment of any rational approach to the problem. To the degree that you can dampen such reactions, scotch rumors, and discourage wild and unfounded speculation, you will be helping mightily to bring things under control. We are not suggesting either falsification or suppression. It is just a good idea to be ready to counterbalance overreactions, and this means a calm and measured response to media questions about death and destruction.

In the case of an ongoing induced catastrophe—such as a kidnapping or hostage/barricade situation—there are extra considerations. Such cases involve negotiations, often delicate and protracted, with human life weighing in the balance. It is important that nothing be said to lead the kidnappers/hostage-takers to conclude that their hostages are more valuable than they had thought (especially if they might be), that you are desperate to get them back (even though we know you are), or that your negotiating position is in any way weaker than they had assumed. In short, you do not want to say anything that might jeopardize your negotiating position or lead the kidnappers/hostage-takers to increase their demands or intransigence. Bear in mind that it is quite likely that anything you say to the press ultimately will reach the ears of the people with whom you are trying to negotiate in one form or another. We recall that in 1973, three diplomats, two Americans and a Belgian were murdered in the Sudan because of an ill-timed comment by President Nixon.[4]

Furthermore, you have to think not only about the current kidnapping or hostage/barricade situation, but also about future incidents. If you are in the sort of business that operates in politically unstable or hostile parts of the world, you must acknowledge the likelihood that there are others out there who are thinking about you and your personnel as potentially attractive targets of opportunity. The statements you make concerning the crisis at hand will ultimately reach would-be terrorists and kidnappers as well. You do not want to say anything that will give them ideas about your general security situation or level of vulnerability. Let them do their own research. Playing down the incident, and its importance to your company or agency, will at least not encourage potential malefactors.[5]

Bear in mind also that terrorism exists mainly for publicity. Groups that destroy property or kidnap hostages usually do so not out of hostility to this officer or that individual, but to have the opportunity to state their case before the court of world public opinion (recall figure 2–1). Whatever the historical legitimacy of the claims and grievances of these various groups, they have in common an inability to make their point of view known. Violence, because it generates publicity, appears to be their best weapon. Almost the entire structure of terrorism rests on a foundation of publicity.

This brings up an interesting philosophical problem. The media have an obligation to the public to report those events they deem newsworthy. But if terrorist attacks were generally ignored, there might very well be fewer of them, since one of the principal reasons for the use of terrorism would then be removed. We do not propose to tackle this difficult quandary here, but, for our purposes, one thing is clear. One of the major reasons for a terrorist action against your organization is the desire for publicity. To the degree that you can control that, you help yourself (and, not coincidentally, the rest of us as well). This is another good reason for downplaying the importance of this type of emergency when talking with reporters.

Unfortunately, this may be easier said than done. In such a situation, there are a number of sources from which you may be pressured to play up the crisis and the importance of a hostage. Family and friends of the victim have a natural interest in calling attention to his or her plight and publicizing their concern. Although this is likely to be detrimental to the ultimate goal of securing the victim's safe release, it can be very difficult to make distraught family members see things from your more dispassionate point of view. And it is nearly impossible to keep them from making their own statements to the press—statements that may question or contradict your own statements or efforts. Witness the continuing efforts of the family and friends of the seven Americans held hostage in Lebanon at the time we write these words.

Similarly, other company or agency employees, as well as family and friends of the victim, may talk to the media for a variety of reasons. Not the least of these, by the way, is the human desire to see their names in print. At least here you have a little more leverage, and we refer you to our earlier discussion of why there should be only one spokesperson dealing with the media.

Finally, other members of the Crisis Action Team may themselves be tempted to say more to journalists than they should, although here the motivation may be a little more complex. A large part of managing a crisis is often just waiting and not taking any action. This may be very necessary, as the team waits for more information, new developments, or a response to a negotiation, but it goes against the grain of many individuals. There is a sense that one ought to be doing *something*, or at least ought to be giving the appearance of doing something. At such times, there is a strong temptation to at least voice one's frustrations if there is a sympathetic journalistic ear around.

For this reason, we want to stress that *only the designated public affairs officer should make public statements,* and *there should be as little contact between the media and the other members of the team as possible.* This has two practical advantages. It frees time for the other members to concentrate on their own responsibilities and it increases the likelihood that the organization will speak with one voice. There are few things worse than having to explain away public contradictions in the middle of an incident. Your job is already hard enough.

If you can't talk about a specific subject, don't. We have already explained at some length why a blanket "no comment" is not likely to be successful. This does not mean, however, that you have to try to handle every single question you might be asked. You will undoubtedly be queried about sensitive policy matters or ticklish situations. The simplest way to handle this is to tell your questioner that this is an area about which you just can't talk. If you are forthcoming and honest in discussing those things you *can* talk about, a competent reporter will understand your situation and not try to back you into a corner. This leaves the question of how to handle an incompetent or unscrupulous reporter, which is much harder. Luckily, such types usually work for papers with small circulations. "No comment" is probably about as well as you can do with a questioner who won't accept that there are some questions you simply can't answer.

If a good reporter believes you are trying honestly to tell him as much as you reasonably can, he or she will generally be more understanding about the off-limits area. He or she may not be completely sympathetic to your situation—remember, reporters have their own job to do—but will respect the parameters you set. Any journalist certainly will prefer this kind of response to a wordy evasion that wastes time and might even be misleading. An example of this sort of cooperation can be found in the 1980 Princes Gate episode. Although a British television channel was filming the scene, the journalists were willing to cooperate with security forces to enhance the chance of success for the rescue operation.

If you don't know the facts, don't talk about the problem. There is no substitute for being prepared, of course, and if you have followed our suggestions you will be. Anticipation and preparation are the keys to effective public affairs management in a crisis. Still, you can't always anticipate everything, and you can count on being asked about at least a few things for which you simply don't have the answers. The simplest response, and the one least likely to do any harm, is the frank admission that you don't know. Above all, *don't speculate.* Good reporters can usually recognize a spongy source, but pressed to come up with some kind of a story and under the gun of a deadline they may decide to go with your speculation—leading to the publication of inaccurate and possibly damaging information. Less-competent reporters may simply assume that you know what you are talking about, with the same results and embarrassment to you personally.

A word or two on the temptation to speculate. It *sounds* easy, reading this book with no crisis on the horizon, to say "I don't know" and avoid unnecessary speculation. In a crisis, however, there are a number of pressures to the contrary. For one thing, let us be honest, this is your moment in the sun. Reporters are asking you, and (if things are being handled correctly) you alone, to comment on the biggest news story of the day. No one wants to appear ignorant under such circumstances. Also, you may be asked a question that you think you *should* be able to answer, and the temptation can be almost overpowering to give it a try. The best advice we can offer is, *don't.* If you are not sure of your facts, don't try to tackle the question.

What we suggest you do is promise to get back to the questioner with some sort of answer as soon as possible. You may be able to refer him to someone who will know the answer, a response which often completely satisfies reporters. Remember, though, that you want to limit media contracts with other members of the team. Referral works best when it is a factual matter that can be answered by someone completely outside your organization. The other alternative is to get the answer yourself and then get back to the questioner. This has the advantage of not only keeping your information factual and accurate, it also scores you points with the media.

Be courteous. On subjects about which you can talk, be as helpful as possible. On those about which you cannot talk, say so frankly. If you can put out a written press statement, do so, making sure that it is reasonably neat and that there are a sufficient number of copies. Keep your cool in the face of annoying and/or repetitive questions. This can be trying when you find yourself answering the same questions over and over again, but that's the nature of the business. It can also be irritating when you have been in the midst of a crisis for hours or days and a reporter demands information on something you can't discuss. Nevertheless, you will best serve yourself and the people for whom you work (not to mention the victim(s), on whose behalf all of this effort is expended) by remaining unfailingly courteous.

Always take or return reporters' calls, even if you know you won't be able to answer his or her questions. This is largely a matter of courtesy, but it also helps to eliminate any impression that you have some reason to avoid the press. As we said before, you want to at least *appear* to know what you are doing. Returning a call just to say "I don't know" or "I can't talk about that" is much better than ignoring the call altogether. The result may be the same, but the impression you create is entirely different. And you may be able to at least deny a rumor that is plain wrong, thereby doing yourself some good.

Establish the ground rules at the beginning of conversation with a reporter. A reporter has the right, or at least may feel that he or she has the right, to assume that whatever you say is for publication unless you agree on the ground rules beforehand. Most good journalists will bring it up themselves, but it is a consideration you should keep firmly in mind any time you talk with the press. There are four bases upon which such conversations can take place that are understood and accepted by all responsible representatives of the media.

1. **On the record.** This means that what you are saying is for publication, and that you do not object to having your name and title used. Generally, it is best to restrict this category to press statements agreed upon and cleared in advance by the Crisis Action Team leader. Beyond that, it is necessary to proceed very carefully. Be aware that reporters generally like to be able to use names and titles, as it lends authority and specificity to their stories. Even an anodyne remark can look bad in print if it is juxtaposed with unfounded speculation from another source (believe us, we know; we've had it done to us). In a crisis, generally limit your "on the record" remarks to previously agreed-upon statements.

2. **Background.** This category and those that follow are less applicable to your function as spokesperson during a crisis, when you presumably be mainly concerned with communicating information on the record. Nonetheless, there will be times when you will find yourself queried by the press—particularly after the resolution of an incident—when these guidelines will be helpful. We leave it to you to decide which is the most appropriate in any given circumstance.

   "Background" is the most common basis on which to talk with newspaper reporters. It allows you to talk about events and policies in a more informal way that you could on the record. *It should not (nor should any of the others) be viewed as a license to speculate inappropriately!* Quotes generally cannot be used, unless you agree to be quoted by name on any particular statement you might make. The general sense of your conversation will be attributed in some way that lends credence without specifically identifying you—for example "department official," "diplomatic source," "industry executive," and so forth. You and the reporter with whom you speak can agree to something beforehand, which can save misunderstanding later on.

3. **Deep background.** This is also a common basis on which to talk to the media. This should be established clearly at the beginning of a conversation, and it means that anything you say can in no way be specifically attributed. Anything used must be prefaced by a statement like, "It is understood that. . ." or "We have learned that. . . ." This allows you greater scope for frankness, but it also puts the reporter in a more difficult position, because he or she will have no visible source for what he or she writes. It is always important to avoid misleading the press, but on "deep background" there is perhaps an extra moral obligation as well.

4. **Off the record.** Technically, this means that a reporter cannot use what you say. The value of such information to a reporter lies in being pointed toward a story, providing something to look into from which a story might result. In most cases, we don't see much advantage in this for you during a crisis; if you can't say something without going "off the record," why say it at all? It isn't likely to do you any good, and it places the reporter in a difficult situation since he or she now has newsworthy information that can't be used. The reporter's job, of course, is to write what he or she knows. In practice, information given off the record rarely stays there.[6] *If you don't want to see it in print, our advice is don't say it.*

Above all, be honest. Honesty really is the best policy in crisis management, if only because of the dangers of being found out. You don't have to tell the media everything you know, but what you do say should be accurate. This applies not only to the literal accuracy of the facts, but to the overall impression you give as well. Don't try to mislead reporters; tell them what you can and don't talk about what you can't. It won't always be easy, but it will do the most good and the least damage in the long run.

PUBLIC AFFAIRS IS A TWO-WAY STREET

An important point to keep in mind is the utility of the media to you. They come to you seeking information, but they also bring quite a bit of their own. Often, in fact, you will get quite a bit more than you give. In the first place, they often have information you don't. This is not surprising when you think about it.

Good reporters will talk to a great many more people than you do in the course of researching a story. They will pick up facts, rumors, speculation, all sorts of things. And they may have enough background material on similar types of stories—other disasters or induced catastrophes, or whatever—to fill in any gaps in your own knowledge. Unlike you, they are quite free to talk about the situation, and most reporters will gladly share what they have learned with you, if you cooperate as much as is possible. They may even want your help in verifying or denying information from another source. Keep your ears open; it is amazing how often you will pick up something useful from a journalist who has come to question you.

During the final days of the Sandinista revolution in Nicaragua and the first days of the new government, one of the authors was stationed in Nicaragua as a political officer. He found that a daily appearance at the Inter-Continental Hotel, if properly timed, would ensure that all the journalists present would share what they had learned that day in exchange for whatever information he could provide. This daily exchange proved profitable for all involved.

The media also, if properly handled, can help you to distribute information or instructions (especially important during an evacuation or for providing warnings), spike rumors, and generally aid your communications. They can also reflect the impression that you seem to know what you are doing—something that can mean good publicity in an otherwise bad situation. In short, handling media inquiries requires tact and delicacy, but if done courteously and intelligently, it can be more than an exercise in damage limitation. It can lead to some positive good.

PUBLIC AFFAIRS MANAGEMENT GUIDELINES

To summarize, the person responsible for the management of public affairs during an emergency should observe the following guidelines:

1. Provide essential, accurate information.
2. Combat the spread of rumors.
3. Avoid premature or unnecessary publicity.
4. Once a crisis is under way, play down the incident as much as possible.
5. Express confidence in those charged with handling the situation, both the authorities and your own Crisis Action Team management.
6. Give regular press briefings and updates, even if you don't have much of substance to add to what is already known.
7. Establish a phone number here you can be reached for information.
8. Establish a designated area to be used for press briefings and interviews.

9. Designate an alternate to fill in if the crisis goes on for an extended period of time. (Loss of continuity or accessibility can lead to the spread of potentially damaging misinformation.)

10. Verify press credentials.

11. Discourage media contact with friends and family of victims and with other employees.

12. Avoid saying anything that might adversely affect other aspects of the Crisis Action Team's job. Even a seemingly unimportant remark can damage negotiations, rescue operations, or government liaison.

13. Avoid inflammatory language; kidnappers and hostage-takers may well have access to newspapers, radio, and television.

SOME FINAL TIPS

DO: Return phone calls.
Establish ground rules in advance.
Try to be sensitive to the media's deadline problems.
Be as accurate and honest as possible.
Keep in mind that the media can be a source of valuable information for you.

DON'T: Try to avoid the media.
Assume that a "no comment" will keep the press from continuing to seek information.
Try to brief the press without adequate preparation and guidelines.
Antagonize media representatives unnecessarily.
Make any statements that you don't want to see on the record.

PUBLIC AFFAIRS MANAGEMENT: A CHECKLIST

✔ Designate a public affairs officer and ensure that he or she is thoroughly familiar with his or her responsibilities and the limitations within which he or she must work.

✔ Ensure that all employees are aware that all media inquiries are to be referred to the public affairs officer and make certain they know who he or she is and where he or she can be reached.

✔ Compile the information that is most likely to be requested by reporters during an emergency and draw up guidelines for its use. Develop statements and answers to questions on subjects you believe will arise in an emergency.

✔ Ensure that the public affairs person is informed immediately of new developments.

✔ Do everything possible to play down the crisis and to avert negative publicity.

✔ **Make certain that an effective working relationship exists between rumor control and the spokesperson.**

✔ Make certain the public affairs person is thoroughly familiar with the ground rules for talking with the press and that these rules are established and in place when he or she talks with the media.

VICTIMS: VISIBLE AND INVISIBLE

8

Shortly before midnight, December 2, 1984, employees at the Union Carbide pesticide plant in the Indian city of Bhopal noticed their eyes were beginning to water. This was apparently not an uncommon experience, as one employee later testified, and nothing was done for about an hour. Internal leaks were generally quite minor, so it was assumed that there need be no particular hurry in this case.

Unfortunately, what the watery eyes indicated this time was a fatal leak of methyl isocyanate (MIC), a gas poisonous not only to the insects for which it is intended, but to human beings as well. It seeped out and enveloped the shanty towns surrounding Bhopal, killing thousands of people and causing serious injury to hundreds of thousands. Whole families—even neighborhoods—were wiped out. For those who didn't die, there was blindness and lung damage. No one knows the full effects of MIC on stillbirths and brain damage, but it is estimated to be considerable. Even worse was the manner in which people died.

MIC reacts violently with water, so the effect of the gas on the lungs was something like drowning. The very young and very old died quickly, but the rest ran through *the dark streets gripped with horror, twitching and gasping for air. It is impossible to know the final total, but most accept that more than two hundred thousand people were seriously affected by the gas.*

For Union Carbide, the worst was still to come. Lawsuits in the billions of dollars were filed as Western lawyers suddenly developed a wholesale interest in the wellbeing of the poverty-stricken people of Bhopal, and more than five hundred thousand claims were filed. (In November 1987, a five-hundred-million-dollar settlement reportedly fell through and the following month the Indian government filed criminal charges against the company and an Indian judge ordered Carbide to make interim relief payments totaling $270 million—about 9 percent of total claims value. Although Union Carbide attributes the leak to a disgruntled employee, the Indian government has charged culpable homicide. The case was expected to come to trial in 1988.) The combination of a public relations catastrophe and massive litigation was devastating to the corporation's financial resources. The price of Union Carbide's stock dropped precipitously and the company was devalued by more than nine hundred million dollars. Crisis management had given way to damage control, and that in turn became a question of corporate survival. The magnitude of this accident, in fact, went far beyond even the immediately obvious—victimizing employees, investors, executives, and even the company itself.

For all its seeming clarity, "victim" is an imprecise term. In emergency situations, it is more often than not difficult to say exactly who are the victims and who are merely bystanders. Obviously, an individual who is taken hostage, or trapped in a hurricane or an earthquake, is a victim. But what about his or her family and friends? His colleagues, who may work under very similar conditions? Or the Crisis Action Team members who may be working around the clock to effect the rescue and whose every decision may result ultimately in life or death? Some speak of "direct" versus "indirect" victims, or "hidden" victims (we have chosen the terms "visible" and "invisible" victims), but any such labels are necessarily going to be awkward. Let's just say that every emergency has a negative and sometimes lasting effect on a lot of people, often in ways that are not at all obvious at first glance.

In this chapter, we want to address ourselves to the needs and problems of the immediate victims; the concerns of those to whom they are important; and the stresses that will be operating on the members of the Crisis Action Team as they struggle with the incident and try to bring it to a successful resolution.[1] Much of what we have to say involves the duration of the crisis itself, but much also applies to that wonderfully long period of time before an emergency occurs. As we have tried to emphasize throughout this book, the hoary adage about prevention and cure is never truer than in crisis management.

Because those directly endangered by the situation are necessarily the focus for everyone else, the logical place to start is with the victim who stands to lose the most—his or her life.

VISIBLE VICTIMS

The better a potential victim is prepared for the possibility of disaster or induced catastrophe, the better the chances of: (a) avoiding it, or (b) successfully coping with the situation once it does arise. Obviously, avoiding trouble is the best course of all, and renders the rest of this book irrelevant. Unfortunately, it is not always possible to do that, but one's chances can be maximized by following a few common-sense precautions. These are applicable in helping to prevent kidnapping, hostage-taking, and ordinary crime. Many unfortunate incidents could be prevented if potential victims would just take the danger seriously and pay attention to a few simple rules.

AVOIDANCE

1. *Keep your car locked.* This helps to cut down on the ease with which it can be stolen; it makes it more difficult for anything to be stolen from it; it discourages people from hiding in the back seat and robbing or kidnapping the driver; and it makes it harder to put anything in the car, like, say, an explosive device. A locked car can still be broken into, of course, but thieves and vandals—and even terrorists—are likely to pass it up for an easier one that isn't locked.

2. *Check your car before getting into it.* This really applies to those who are living in high-risk areas. Most people tend to feel a bit foolish looking under their car before they unlock it, but it is not a joking matter. Recent years have seen a rise in the incidence of car bombs, and even a locked car is vulnerable. Anyone parking in an unsecured area in a country where terrorism exists should make it a habit to give his or her car a quick inspection before opening it and starting the engine.

3. *Vary your route and, if possible, your times of arrival and departure.* This also applies to those in high-risk areas and it is also something which many people treat as a joke. Terrorists and criminal kidnappers, however, have to be able to count on the predictability of their targets' movements, and anything that makes a potential victim less predictable helps to avert such incidents. A remarkably high percentage of kidnappings—and quite a few assassinations—have been accomplished while the victim was en route somewhere in his car (often between work and home).

4. *Travel main raods.* Often, the more people around, the harder it is for anyone to commit an illegal act. Kidnappings and assassinations are possible on any road, but they are a lot easier to bring off in deserted areas.

5. *Travel with others when possible.* In general, there is safety in numbers. Two people together are normally less likely to be attacked than is one person alone.

6. *Do not frequent high-risk areas.* Many of the most serious incidents that have taken place abroad have occurred because the victims were somewhere they shouldn't have been. This is good advice anywhere. If an area is known to be dangerous, and there is no compelling reason to go there, *stay away from it!*

7. *Do not advertise your schedule and do not give personal information to strangers.* As in number three, less predictable people make harder targets.

8. *Maintain a list of emergency telephone numbers.* The largest part of managing a crisis is being prepared for it. You don't want to be trying to find the fire department's telephone number in the midst of a fire. Doctor, ambulance, police and fire departments, and so forth, should all have their telephone numbers recorded legibly somewhere handy to the telephone. Phone numbers of your spouse's workplace and your children's school(s) should also be readily available.

9. *Report anything suspicious.* This is one of the most important of all. Inquiries from strangers, prowlers, an individual hanging around over a period of time with no apparent reason for being in the vicinity, an unidentified vehicle parked in an area where it does not belong—all of these may have perfectly innocent explanations, but they also may be signs of trouble. People generally do not like to report such things, fearing that they will look foolish if what they have seen does not turn out to be an indication of criminal or terrorist activity. On the other hand, many victims of kidnapping and assassination attempts, to say nothing to robberies, have later bemoaned the fact that they had noticed something suspicious beforehand but had done nothing about it. In areas where the individual has reason to consider himself or herself a potential target, it is much better to err on the side of caution. A lot of very serious problems can be prevented if you keep your eyes open and report what you see to the proper officials.

PREPARATION

Even where averting a crisis is impossible, there are still enormous benefits to be had from proper preparation on the part of the potential victim. Concerns that normally seem mundane can assume overpowering proportions for an individual in a life-threatening situation. Some of what comes next may seem a bit odd, but human psychology tends to be quirky under any circumstances, and emergencies will exacerbate that tendency. Victims who have seen to all the mundane preparations we suggest will be in a far stronger psychological position that those who have not.

In the 1950s, Vance Packard, in *The Hidden Persuaders,* noted that an airline study had found that a number of executives were afraid to fly—not because they feared death, but because they hated the thought of looking foolish if they did get killed in a plane crash. That is, they hated to think of their surviving loved ones standing around saying, "I told him to take the train," or "Didn't he know that airline had a poor safety record?" This makes no objective sense, of course, but it is very human. In much the same way, victims in an emergency situation are likely to be assailed by a number of troubling thoughts—not only, "My God, I might die!" but also "The rent's due today and Mary doesn't know where I keep the checkbook." In fact, it has been found again and again that one of the biggest problems for hostages in terrorist incidents is the overwhelming sense of guilt they feel at not having made all the necessary arrangements for their families.

The victim of a kidnapping or hijacking, and to a lesser extent, of a disaster (if it is prolonged over a period of hours or days), will have a much easier time coping with his or her situation if he or she is not plagued by guilt about seemingly routine and trivial matters. Confinement and powerlessness are bad enough under any circumstances, but they are infinitely worse if compounded by a sense of worry over all the things left undone. We recommend that employees be briefed thoroughly on this aspect of potential crises—as a general principle for everyone and most particularly for those who may be about to be transferred into any areas of potential danger. The following suggestions might be scoffed at or postponed in the absence of danger, but those who follow the advice will be very glad if an emergency develops.

1. Important documents should be stored in a safe deposit box or similar repository, and the location of their storage should be known to those friends and family members who may need them. It may also be a good idea to make copies of such papers and leave them with an attorney. Copies should also be kept at home, in the event of a situation where a spouse needs immediate access and the safe deposit box is in another city or country. Documents will vary from person to person, of course, but the following are the kinds of things that should be included: personal will, birth certificate, marriage license, power of attorney, financial papers, insurance papers, tax records, medical records, dental records, and school transcripts.

   In addition, a list of all credit card numbers should be drawn up, along with a list of all financial holdings (with fund or brokerage names and account numbers), and copies of whatever else may be relevant in the particular case: divorce decrees, adoption papers, naturalization papers, or whatever. It may also be useful to have a joint bank account into which salary can be deposited and from which your family can withdraw money. This can save an enormous number of headaches for family members during a protracted emergency. Anything else that can be foreseen, no matter how seemingly simple—names and phone numbers of doctors, pediatricians, auto mechanics, and so on—

should be included. The better prepared you are, the less there is to worry about if trouble comes.

2. Every adult should have a will drawn up. This is a difficult point to sell people on, because a will means acknowledging that you are going to die, and no one likes to think too long about that. Even in the best of times, many people postpone making arrangements for the disposition of their property after their demise, preferring not to face the inevitable. At the onset of a possibly dangerous transfer, they are doubly reluctant, since they often really don't want to acknowledge the added danger. Nonetheless, this is one of the most serious worries people have when confronted with the possibility of their own death. Most wills require very little time or effort and are relatively inexpensive. They can mean vastly less psychological stress for crisis victims, both actual and potential. And, like it or not, it's something that will have to be done sooner or later by all of us.

3. Insurance should be up to date. This applies to every type of insurance: automobile, mortgage, household effects, medical, disability, and life. Policies should be reviewed periodically, a list compiled of policy types, premium amounts, due dates for payments, agents' names, and so forth, and all of this information should be kept along with the policies themselves in a safe place—copies having been made and accessibly stored. Life insurance represents a particular problem for some people because, like a will, it involves facing the prospect of one's own mortality. Nonetheless, an individual in a life-threatening situation will gain considerable solace, and suffer less stress, if he or she has provided adequately for the family's future.

4. It is a good idea to compile as complete an inventory of possessions as possible, again with copies in safe places. This is not only handy for the peace of mind of victims of an ongoing situation, but also can be extremely useful in case of more conventional disasters. A fire or hurricane can destroy many thousands of dollars' worth of possessions in a matter of minutes. A victim can then spend months or years trying to figure out everything that was lost, establish the total value, and recoup the loss. Lists like this can be a lot of work, but they are well worth the effort in the event of an emergency. Photographs are also helpful.

The inventory should include furniture, clothing, jewelry, and any items of special value, such as paintings or stamp collections. It should include, as far as is possible, a description of each item, the date of its purchase, the purchase price, and its current market and/or replacement value. This may be more work than most people will care to do, but we recommend that at least those items of major value be catalogued and periodically updated. The list can be written, photographed, tape-recorded, video-recorded, kept on a floppy disk, or any combination of these methods. It is an especially good idea to have photographs of paintings, jewelry, and hobby items of special value. Again, keep copies of your lists and photographs in a safe place.

5. Financial matters should be arranged as efficiently as possible. Checkbooks and bankbooks should be secure and accessible, and family members should know where they are and how to get to them. It is also a good idea to have some ready cash at hand in case of emergency (even if it's not a full-blown crisis). Traveler's checks are useful for this, since they combine availability, negotiability, and security. There should be a few checks in each spouse's name, to prevent a situation in which the only person who can cash them is the one who is unavailable to sign them. A small amount of cash in a safe place is also a good idea.

   For married couples, a joint checking account is also highly recommended. It is hard to imagine a more frustrating situation than a spouse with bills to pay and a full, unusable checkbook. It is even worse if regular paychecks are deposited into an untouchable account, as is the case for many employees. For the same reason, we also recommend that each adult family member have his or her own credit card. Finally, in cases where employees are assigned abroad, all credit and check cashing arrangements should be worked out in advance.

6. In addition to all of the foregoing, the cache of documents and important papers should include: résumés, reference letters, passport numbers, drivers' license numbers, car registration data, medical prescriptions, and anything else of which the individual may be able to think. There is no such thing as too much information. If no emergencies arise, these things are still nice to have in one place. If the worst comes to pass, they can make all the difference.

7. Lastly, but far from least, these things should be gone over within the family. Every family member should know what is expected of him or her in an emergency, where things are and what needs to be done. Such discussions not only serve the obvious function of making a difficult situation easier in a crisis, they also help to prepare family members psychologically should such a situation develop.

All this can do a lot to set a victim's mind at rest and ease somewhat his or her ordeal during a prolonged emergency. The individual must know about these steps and then be convinced to take them. It is the responsibility of a company or other employer to make sure that its people know about these things. This not only makes life easier for everyone involved in a crisis, but it may also help to preclude subsequent lawsuits for negligence. Convincing employees that these steps are necessary can be a trial, however, sometimes because the idea frightens them too much for them to be willing to think about the possibilities. Before going on to the other aspects of victimology, we would like to say a few words about briefing potential victims and getting them to attend to the briefer's recommendations.

THE SECURITY BRIEFING

Ultimately, some employees are going to be interested and some are not, some are going to take the warnings to heart and some are not, and some are going to be frightened while others will remain unaffected. No briefer is ever going to have total success with any audience, but a few of the following principles may at least increase the briefer's chances of success.

The briefer should be perceived as an expert in his subject. A team of experts is even better, if that can be arranged. An audience of potential victims tends to be resistant to warnings and suggested precautions as a form of denial. If the person issuing the warnings is someone who is seen as having been there, who knows what he or she is talking about, then the briefing has a better chance of making an impression. This is, by the way, easier said than done. A recitation of old war stories tends to bore people quickly, losing the point of the message. A good security briefer has to establish his credentials quickly and succinctly, without burdening his audience with his own autobiography. Often this can be done by the person introducing the briefer, leaving the expert free to concentrate on the advice.

The briefer should anticipate and deal with some of the likely negative reactions. A lot of recommended security precautions—taking different routes to work, looking under a car before getting into it, and other such standard procedures—seem to the average person as inconvenient, excessive, and paranoiac. Indeed, many of the recommendations made in the first part of this chapter may have already struck some readers as overkill. A good briefer will acknowledge up front that a certain amount of effort will be required to get these things done, that some false alarms will result, and that an individual does occasionally run the risk of appearing foolish if his or her fears turn out to be groundless. (It has been our experience that many people seem to be more afraid of looking foolish than of being killed or kidnapped.) These points conceded, it should be emphasized that the precautions are still very much worth taking because the results of ignoring the warnings can be so terrible and far-reaching.

After acknowledging the objections, the next question is how to get the attendees' attention. Danger in the abstract is moderately interesting, and worth thinking about on a quiet day. Danger to oneself, on the other hand, is a matter of the most immediate and intense concern. Most people tend to see a threat in very personal terms, such as are *they* likely to be affected, and what will it mean if they ignore the warnings they are being given? It is important to personalize the threat as much as possible, an argument for small briefing groups rather than large ones, whenever this is feasible. The briefer should always bear in mind that each member of the audience is going to follow the advice only to the degree of perceived threat to self or loved ones.

Unfortunately, this leads directly to a major difficulty. A briefer has to make the listeners aware of the dangers they might have to face, but if he or she scares them too much, the denial response may be provoked. Unwilling to accept the reality of the potential threat level, many people will simply resent the briefer for using "scare tactics" and they will tune out the rest of the message. They will return quickly to the reservations expressed earlier, assuring themselves that it can't really be that bad and that the briefer is probably a very unpleasant and excitable individual. These reactions are very common, for example, in the many briefings given to U.S. government employees assigned overseas. Our experience suggests that these reactions can be overcome.

There are three ways of approaching this problem. The briefer can offer the warnings and discuss precautions, but play down the danger; or he can talk about the danger, discuss security measures, but avoid specifics; or he can be very specific as to the degree and type of danger that the audience may have to face, and the precautions which they should take. This last risks scaring the squeamish and possibly turning people off, but we believe it to be by far the best approach, with a few caveats.

As to the first approach, there isn't much point in trying to prepare people for potential danger if the risks of the situation are played down. People are only too prepared already to deny a threatening situation, and they are mostly looking for reassurance that everything will be all right. Because the chief purpose of a security briefing is to prevent complacency and to put people on their guard, playing down the danger is, to say the least, counterproductive. Obviously, we are not advocating scare tactics, but a certain amount of self-interested fear is necessary to motivate potential victims to take the kinds of precautions that are designed to keep them from becoming victims in the first place.

The second approach is even worse. If people are frightened, without anything definite upon which to focus, the result will be merely heightened anxieties, greater stress, and a kind of paralysis. Rumors may get started, usually much worse than anything the real world has to offer. Employees may become less productive, suffer more stress, and yet not really be motivated to take the steps—like making a will or thinking about life insurance—that force them to confront the unpleasant things they would rather deny. A discussion of security precautions in such a context will be largely meaningless, because some people will not understand the importance or applicability of the recommendations if they do not comprehend the nature of the threat.

We believe the best approach is the most specific: potential victims should be told of the danger, its likely source (so far as is known), what can be done to avoid or ameliorate it, and the likely consequences of not doing so. This last is the part that scares people and can provoke denial, but if done correctly it is well worth that risk. A trip to the dentist is less stressful if the patient knows exactly what the dentist is going to do, what to expect, and what would happen if the problem were allowed to go untreated. The same is true for shots, surgery, and, on a larger scale, potential disasters.

In fact, fear seems to work a little like a vaccine. A very weak case of a disease, which is what a vaccine is, mobilizes the body's immune system and protects it against more virulent forms of that disease. Similarly, a small amount of concerned self-interest, with a clear understanding of recommended precautions, seems to help when a full-blown crisis materializes. Having been warned that such situations can occur, the victim is taken less by surprise and can begin to function in a productive manner much more quickly. A programmed response is more likely to be activated, and the victim is much less likely to feel overwhelmed by the event.

The trick is, of course, to make potential victims sit up and take notice without terrifying them—easy to talk about, but more difficult to do. We recommend presenting not only the consequences, but also the statistical rate of occurrence of these types of incidents (see Appendix A). It is important that an audience know the odds are against anything like this happening to any of them, but a certain number of these events will occur every year and they would be foolish not to be prepared for them.[2] The idea is to make people aware, and to get them to take the briefer's advice, not to scare them off completely.

If potential victims do not heed the recommendations presented in a security briefing it is generally for one of three reasons: they do not see it as applying to them personally, they do not think it is worth the time and/or trouble, or they are afraid of looking silly and/or paranoid. There is no certain way to avoid one or more of these reactions, but we offer the following suggestions.

1. Be sure the sense and nature of the danger is unequivocal. These are things that *do* happen and they *can* happen to members of your audience.

2. Support this assertion with specifics—facts, statistics, and anecdotes as appropriate. Be careful not to overdo it, though. If the audience gets bored by a recitation of statistics or incidents, it may tune out and miss the important part of the message.

3. Recommendations should be as specific as possible, and tied to the presentation of the threat. "There were X number of electrical fires in this area last year, all attributed to faulty aluminum wiring, and that is why you should have the wiring checked in your home. Here is how it should be done (along with some of the unpleasant results of *not* doing it)."

4. Show concern without a sense of pressure and anxiety. The idea to convey is that these are dangers with which we have to live, they are serious but not unheard of, and they can be minimized by the application of some care and common sense. A failure to take reasonable precautions is likely to be damaging.

5. Follow the presentation with (or incorporate into it) an opportunity for questions and answers. Treat all questions seriously. People will ask some pretty weird questions, but the very process of involving them makes their compliance more likely. Besides, as our mothers always told us as children, there are no stupid questions, only stupid answers.

6. Try to show your expertise without coming across as pompous or pedantic. Try to be entertaining without seeming flip. These are tall orders, but an important element in any sort of briefing. The better the audience likes the presenter, the more they can relate to him or her, the more likely they are to receive the message and to follow the briefer's advice.

SURVIVAL TECHNIQUES

Preparation for a crisis means more than inventories and wills and safety precautions, however. Besides getting one's house in order in advance, and learning how to recognize and/or to avoid threatening situations, a potential victim must also have some idea of what to expect should the worst come to pass. In the case of fire, theft, and most disasters, this relates to what can be expected after the incident has taken place. In the case of kidnappings, hostage-taking, or airline hijackings, however, there is a period of time—sometimes quite substantial—that represents the actual incident. It is neither preparation for nor recovery from, but those terrible hours, days, weeks, or even longer, when the incident is taking place. During this time, a hostage or kidnapping victim will be under the most intense and psychologically destructive pressure, and his or her response may be the difference between survival intact on the one hand, and severe emotional or physical damage, even death, on the other.

There is a considerable quantity of excellent literature on hostage situations and victimology (see examples in the bibliography), and it is not our purpose to reproduce it here. The aim of this chapter is to offer some suggestions for preparing potential victims for the kind of crisis situations in which they may find themselves, along with some advice for those who will have to deal with these victims during and after an incident. A great deal of research suggests that the pressure on hostages will be less if they have some idea of what to expect and have been able to accept the situation in advance. Toward that end, we want to discuss the general characteristics of a hostage-taking or a kidnapping as they relate to the victim, leaving aside the very real objective differences between these types of incidents. We will also cover the key points for victims to bear in mind once they have emerged from the crisis alive and, optimally, unharmed.

Hostage and kidnapping situations vary greatly, depending in large part on the mental states and motivations of the perpetrators, but there are several constants that can be expected in just about every situation. The critical one, the one from which all other reactions and alternatives flow, is the fact that *the victim has lost control of his or her destiny.* The most basic decisions of existence—whether he or she can move around or must remain in one place, whether he or she may speak or must remain silent, whether he or she can go to the bathroom—will be made by someone else. And, at the bottom of it all, the decision as to whether he or she will live or die is no longer under the victim's control.

A crisis of this magnitude calls into question practically everything that is fundamental to a human being. Dehumanization, total dependence on the good will of one's captor, the sense of one's own helplessness—all of these can be very damaging psychologically. A victim must not only avoid being killed or maimed in such a situation, but also must be able to maintain enough personal dignity to remain unscarred by the experience once it has ended. It is a very precarious balance for any human being—too much resistance may mean death, too little may mean severe psychological damage that will last for many years. No one can lay down a blueprint for proper behavior in every situation of this type. But if a victim has some idea beforehand of what to expect, not only in the treatment he or she will receive, but also in the natural emotional reactions to that treatment, he or she will have a much better chance of responding appropriately, in ways that will cause the least likelihood of harm. As we have said again and again throughout this book, the more that can be anticipated, the better the emergency can be handled. This is, if anything, even truer for the victim of a hostage-taking or kidnapping.

The first emotional reaction a normal person is likely to have is blind fear, even panic. It is useful to be aware of this in advance, since a few moments of panic can lead to behavior the victim may find hard to "live down" afterward. A normally brave man or woman may respond to a sudden alarm by screaming, or running blindly, or in ways that are even less creditable. When reason returns, as it nearly always does after a few seconds or minutes, the individual may feel intensely embarrassed and, consequently, demoralized. Since morale is one of the key factors in surviving this type of situation, such a reaction is counterproductive. Potential hostages should be given to understand that panic is a normal response to a suddenly threatening environment; it is better avoided, but it is nothing of which to be ashamed.

Immediate panic is usually superseded by denial: "This isn't possible, it can't be happening." This may manifest itself in withdrawal, refusal to accept the reality of the situation, sleepiness, or, surprisingly, a transfer of the hostage's fear from the captor to the police, the famous Stockholm Syndrome. One form it may take is in the unreasoning belief that rescue is imminent. The problem with this is that, as the hours lengthen and rescue does not occur, the disappointment can be crushing psychologically. Denial, turning inward, is probably a healthy response at this point.

Circumstances vary too much from one incident to another to lay down too many rules. There may be many captives or just one, they may be grouped together or isolated, they may be bound, blindfolded, stripped and beaten, asked to sign statements or "confessions"—it depends on the nature of the incident and the motivation of the captors. Physical and psychological pressures may be greater or lesser, but, in order to survive, the hostage will have to walk a fine line between resistance and compliance. Overcompliance can be as bad as over-resistance, and the victim in this situation has to make all decisions under the most intense pressure. Within these parameters, we offer a few suggestions, based upon personal experience and the studies that are available.

1. *Don't call attention to yourself.* People who take captives are often unstable, and especially so during the initial hours of an incident. This is particularly true in unplanned hostage situations, like those resulting from a foiled robbery, for example, but it is true enough in any event. Any attention that may be directed to a hostage is not likely to be favorable. Verbal abuse or violence may very well occur and, if captors begin selecting hostages for execution, those who have drawn notice are generally the first to go.

   Obviously, this doesn't apply when there are only one or two victims or hostages.[3] But there are a great many situations involving large numbers of hostages—hijackings and embassy takeovers, for example. If you find yourself in such a spot, the basic rule is to keep your head down.

2. *Keep as busy and active as the circumstances allow.* We are talking here mainly about *mental* activity, although any opportunities for physical exercise should be taken. One of the problems in a prolonged hostage situation is the often cramped, claustrophobic atmosphere it can create for the victim. Stretching and flexibility exercises, isometrics, even jogging in place, are all good ideas; they occupy the mind, stimulate the circulation, keep muscles from cramping, and help keep up morale. All of this is recommended, of course, if it can be done without contravening the first rule.

   Mental activity is extremely important. The environment is unpleasant enough without forcing the mind to dwell on the dangers and discomforts. As we have said before, a certain amount of withdrawal is probably a healthy thing. The literature is rich with stories of hostages and prisoners of war who designed computer circuits, compiled dictionaries, planned houses, and undertook—if only in their minds—many equally complex projects.[4] It doesn't much matter what the activity is. Name all the World Series winners. List all the Gene Autry movies you can think of. Start the novel you've been planning to write. Design your dream house. Whatever it is, if it occupies your mind it will go a long way toward keeping up your morale and increasing your chances of surviving with as little psychological damage as is possible.

3. *Don't complain.* It calls attention to yourself, it annoys the captors and makes violent and unstable behavior more likely on their part, and it lowers group morale. It also doesn't do much for your own morale and self-image. We

realize a hostage situation is very unpleasant and trying, and that there is occasional value in gently asserting your dignity, but a hostage should be aware that this kind of behavior is not likely to accomplish much and can have highly negative results.

4. *Don't confront or anger captors.* Occasionally one reads of former hostages who report that they challenged or humiliated their captors, or that they dazzled them with the logic of their arguments, confusing them and making them doubt their purpose. If these stories are true, they have our admiration, but we do not recommend it as a means of increasing your chances of survival. Generally, the hostage who threatens his or her captors, who identifies himself or herself by the force of arguments or actions as a potential problem, is one of the first chosen for execution if the captors feel they need to demonstrate their seriousness of purpose. It is important to retain one's sense of dignity and self-worth in a situation of this type, but those things won't be worth much if you fail to survive the incident.

Much has been made of the Stockholm Syndrome, of which we will say more shortly. But there is also a reaction sometimes called the London Syndrome, which clearly illustrates this point. During the takeover of the Iranian Embassy in London in 1980, there was a hostage named Abbas Lavasani, an articulate supporter of the fundamentalist regime in Iran. He insisted on arguing with his captors, and, as they were somewhat less trained in rhetorical skills than he was, he won most of the arguments. Unfortunately, they solved the problem by killing him and heaving his body into the street. Forceful resistance when you are a hostage is a quick way to reduce the chances of your survival.

5. *Don't overcomply.* First, because this can get you killed too, and second, because you have to live with yourself afterward. As to the first, we have already mentioned the dangers of drawing attention to yourself. Oddly enough, overcompliance is as much a violation of that rule as verbal abuse or physical resistance. In postincident interviews, captors have said that they had intended this or that hostage for the first execution "because he was such a wimp" (or words to that effect).[5] Sycophancy may not seem like all that bad of an idea under the circumstances (it may be an act of psychological regression for some), but it can get you killed.

The other problem with too much compliance is the same as that which we noted about the initial panic reaction. It can be the source of considerable loss of self-worth later on. Being a captive is a degrading experience that leaves its own scars. Feeling that you have cooperated in the degradation is even worse. As far as possible, a hostage or kidnap victim should try to lose himself or herself in comfortable, dignified behavior, performing routines that are familiar and pleasant. Keep the mind occupied and try not to attract any special notice. We are aware this advice is much easier said than done, but those individuals who have come through prolonged hostage situations in the best shape are the ones who have followed this advice.

The Stockholm Syndrome is a rather common reaction in hostage situations, particularly prolonged ones, and it is something of which a potential victim should be aware. The syndrome gets its name from an incident in a Stockholm bank in August 1973. Four hostages were imprisoned in the bank's vault for 131 hours, during which time they were totally dependent on their captors for survival. By the time they were released, they had transferred all their sympathies to the people who had been holding them hostage, and had convinced themselves that it was the criminals who had been protecting them from the police.[6]

It is difficult to say precisely what the psychological reasons are for this reaction. It may be a form of regression, growing out of the sense of total dependence upon one's captors (not unlike the total dependence of an infant on its parents); it may be an overwhelming need to connect with other human beings in the presence of the threat of death, even if those others are the cause of the threat; or it may be some sort of perverse identification with authority under extreme stress. Whatever the reasons, the result is the paradoxical situation of hostages' sympathizing with the people responsible for their plight and resenting the efforts of those trying to rescue them. This reaction can persist for quite a while after the incident has ended. (One of the victims in the Stockholm bank robbery later married one of her captors.) Former hostages have reported continuing positive feelings for their captors, even while they experience nightmares and phobias about those very people escaping and coming after them again.

A hostage will be better able to deal with this paradox if he or she knows in advance that it is a normal psychological response to a highly abnormal situation. All such reactions, from preliminary panic to subsequent nightmares, are easier to tolerate if potential victims are aware of and understand them in advance of an incident. In this case, there is an added benefit, and it relates to what we consider the most important element in the whole matter of hostage survival.

6. *Try to have your captors to see you as a real person.* Hostages begin as nothing more than faceless symbols to their captors. They are seen as either representatives of some policy of their government that the hostage-takers don't like (even though the hostages may have nothing whatever to do with that policy and in fact may not even have heard of it), or pawns to be sacrificed in the negotiations for their own release (in the case of a barricade situation), or possibly both. Many people who find themselves holding hostages are, oddly enough, not the sort of hardened criminals who unconcernedly can commit murder. They *will* murder hostages, however, as long as they have not begun to think of them as anything other than symbols or pawns.

Invariably, when a hostage situation is prolonged, and captors and hostages begin to know each other as people, a subtle change comes over them. We have already talked about the Stockholm Syndrome and it is not a one-way street.

Symbols are easy to eliminate. Flesh-and-blood human beings, with spouses and children and friends, are not. Again and again, criminals and even professional terrorists have chosen not to harm their captives, *once they got to know them*. People living together in close quarters, under pressure, for a prolonged time, will usually develop a certain psychological bond, even between terrorists and their prisoners. This can be made to work to the advantage of the hostage, increasing the chance of survival.

Figure 8–1 summarizes the important points made here. There is a certain tension among some of these points. How, for example, does one not call attention to oneself, yet be seen as a human being? It is impossible to be much more specific, given the differences in every situation. But the general principles remain the same. A hostage who can avoid drawing negative attention, and yet can exploit the affinity that tends to grow between captor and captive over time, has a vastly increased chance of survival with psyche intact. Along these lines, we offer the rapport-building suggestions shown in figure 8–2 for your consideration.

Avoid Calling Special Attention to Yourself

Keep Busy Mentally and Physically

Do Not Resist Physically

Avoid Overcompliance

Maintain Your Dignity and Self-respect

Make Your Captors Aware that You are a Person

Figure 8–1. Important Survival Points for Potential Hostages

BUILDING RAPPORT

Building rapport with captors is an important self-defense action a hostage can and should undertake. It may be helpful to think of rapport-building as a bank account and the techniques noted below as deposits to that account. The whole idea is to build up the balance as rapidly and as greatly as possible so that it will be large enough for later withdrawals that may mean the difference between survival and death. As an incident develops, the captors will have choices to make about releasing hostages, killing them, surrendering, etc. These decisions

TECHNIQUE	EFFECT
Listen carefully	Calming influence
Personalize dialogue	Humanizes situation
	Builds bonds
Empathize, don't criticize	Demonstrates understanding
	Improves climate
	Promotes trust
Be creative	Overcomes glitches
	Solves problems
Avoid lying	Destroys climate/trust
Be consistent	Promotes predictability
	Reinforces trust
Be responsive	Enhances bonding

Figure 8–2. How To Build Rapport with Your Captors

will be influenced by the degree of rapport an individual captive has developed; you might say, by the size of the bank balance.

We have already mentioned the importance of not confronting or challenging your captors. This does not preclude your paying attention to what is said and done around you. As a matter of fact, a simple and effective technique in almost any situation is to listen carefully to what is said to you. This not only helps you understand what is happening, it also serves as a calming influence on persons who might be haranguing you emotionally.

Another important tool available to you is to personalize whatever contact occurs between you and your captors. By exploiting every contact with your captors as an opportunity to demonstrate that you are a person and not a mere symbol you will greatly increase your chances of survival. Family pictures, or acting with calm dignity, have been used successfully by hostages in past incidents.

If your captors choose to discuss their reasons for having made you their hostage, there is nothing wrong with indicating that you can understand why these reasons impelled them to undertake such an action. This does not mean that you express agreement with their politics or other rationale; rather, you once again demonstrate that you are a thinking, caring individual—a person, not a thing. This will often encourage further contacts between you and improve the climate and level of trust in your relationship. All of this will work to your benefit. In July 1979, one of the authors was taken prisoner for a brief period by one of the numerous militia groups which had sprung up during the toppling of the Somoza government. Many of the suggestions we make here proved useful then.

When you have the chance, be creative. Many times an unanticipated problem will arise or a glitch of some sort will develop. If you can be part of the solution, you will demonstrate not only that you are a thinking person, but also that you are indispensable to your captors.

Above all, avoid lying. No matter how successful you have been in establishing a level of trust and rapport, one lie can undo it all. You can protect vital information and/or avoid embarassment without lying. One important corollary to this is to be consistent in your responses to your captors. This will promote predictability and reinforce whatever level of trust may be the result of your efforts.

Finally, be responsive. If you are spoken to, answer. You needn't volunteer information nor need you be disputatious. However, if you refuse to engage in a dialogue with your captors, you are no different from the wall and you cannot hope to engender the type of rapport that may be required to save your life.

READJUSTMENT AFTERWARD

There is a tendency for the general public to think about emergency situations only in terms of preparation and survival. Once the ordeal is "over," we tend to think of the matter as fully resolved and we are ready to get on with something else. Unfortunately, this is not the case for former hostages or, often, for those who have survived earthquakes, hurricanes, and similar disasters. Nor is this necessarily the case for family or even colleagues of the victim. There is often a long period of readjustment that follows even the most successful resolution of an emergency, and those responsible for the wellbeing of victims will have their work cut out for them. While reactions will vary according to the duration and type of emergency and the nature of the individual, there are certain patterns which can be expected.

First, immediately upon release or rescue, victims (especially of hostage or kidnapping situations) may be very distrustful and withdrawn (children may refuse to be separated from parents). Perhaps this is the other side of the denial response; having had difficulty accepting the reality of the previous situation, a victim may have trouble readjusting to the reality of freedom or rescue. This is especially true if a number of hopes during the incident were disappointed. This can be a problem in dealing with those who are anxious to welcome him or her back and expect high spirits and jubilation. It can be especially hard on family members who have only been through the experience from the outside and cannot understand or accept the victim's continued withdrawal.

It is extremely important to shield the victim from well-meaning sympathizers, curious individuals, opportunistic politicians, and the media. The media have their own agendas, of course, but a just-released victim is in no emotional state to handle that right away. Should an interview be given, things may be said that will be regretted later. Consider, for example, a hostage still under the influence of the Stockholm Syndrome, talking about the people who have worked to free him or her. It is not uncommon for former hostages to angrily criticize the people who most deserve their gratitude and praise those who most deserve their rancor. No one should be put in that position or be allowed to put him self or herself in that position until there has been an opportunity to readjust to reality.

The aftermath of the TWA 847 hijacking in June 1985 is a good example of this. In that case, the media had become a pawn of the terrorists and little could be done to prevent it. Much bitterness grew up among the hostages because of some comments made in the heat of the moment.

Another reason for limiting visitors is that victims may be suffering from sleep deprivation and/or emotional exhaustion. The emergency, which is traumatic enough, is followed by the considerable commotion attendant upon the release or rescue. Victims are reunited with their loved ones, who have been through their own emotional ordeal, pushed and pulled in every direction and the center of attention. It is not surprising that so many suffer from sensory overload and appear disoriented. Physical examinations and debriefings are necessary, and it is best that these take place in a controlled environment, where victims will not be further overwhelmed by the questions and demands of well-meaning (and sometimes not-so-well-meaning) spectators.

Debriefings serve a dual purpose: they allow authorities the opportunity to extract needed information, and they provide an outlet for victims to blow off some steam. The latter can be psychologically therapeutic, but it is best done well away from public eyes. This is especially the case when some victims have been released or rescued but others are still at risk and the situation has not yet been completely resolved. Public remarks have to be very carefully weighed and someone only recently released or rescued is not likely to be the best judge of such things. It is best for debriefings to be held in a restful and private location. Hospitals are a good choice, because access can be controlled and the debriefing can be combined with the necessary physical examinations. This was the approach employed after the January 1981 release of the fifty-four Americans held captive at the U.S. Embassy in Tehran, Iran.

If a hospital or similar medical setting is chosen, however, it is important that victims not be treated as though they were regular patients. The aim of a rehabilitation plan is to return the victims to a normal life as smoothly and quickly as possible. Treating them like ordinary patients tends to complicate this process. During the hospital stay, released hostages should be allowed to wear their own clothes, move around freely, and generally behave as normally as possible, consistent with the needs of the debriefing, medical attention, and access limitation.

They should also be allowed to talk to each other as freely as possible. This will provide an excellent opportunity to talk out some of their feelings, share experiences, and compare some of their reactions. Feelings that disturb an individual will be much easier to accept if others in the same circumstances express similar reactions. And communication with other victims also provides just about the only opportunity for people who have been through an essentially unique experience to unburden themselves to others who can be expected to understand. One of the biggest problems some former hostages have is trying to explain their experience or their feelings about that experience to someone who wasn't there. No matter how well doctors or psychologists are trained, a survivor of an experience like this may well feel that only another survivor can really understand what he or she is talking about.

After the initial round of media attention, the public tends to go on to other things, but it is at this point that victims' real readjustment problems begin. Naturally this will depend on the length of the period of captivity and the internal resources of the victim, but certain patterns of behavior may emerge even after a relatively short incident. These are things of which not only the victim must be made aware, but also family, friends, and employers.

There is a tendency for the victim to "make up" for deprivations caused by the emergency. This is more typical of situations following a long period of captivity. A former hostage has missed out on a lot of things and may be tempted to go overboard in compensating. Having lived for a time with the specter of death, he or she may experience difficulty in limiting the things he or she wants. This is particularly a problem when a former hostage has some back pay coming, or a relatively large sum of money in some other form. He or she may at first be tempted to overspend or sink the money into doubtful investments. Similarly, he or she may overeat, gaining a considerable amount of weight in a short period of time. Suddenly being able to do as he or she pleases after a prolonged period of limitation may lead the victim to do a number of inadvisable things. Adequate counseling at the outset may help forestall some of this.

There is also sometimes a tendency on the part of former hostages to make up for all the deprivations they perceive (rightly or wrongly) their families have suffered. They sometimes blame themselves for any problems the family had during their absence, which loads them with extra guilt, on top of all their other psychological problems. They may try to compensate for this by overindulging children, smothering loved ones with attention and affection, and generally trying to provide everything all at once. Because families have also been through a period of separation, they may have their own adjustments to make, and this can be trying for everyone. Again, this is generally truer when the captivity has been lengthy.

In general, it is a good idea for victims to return to work as soon as they are fit. Prolonged vacations do not seem to have a beneficial effect, although a little time off is all right. The best thing for a former hostage is to get back into a "normal" routine as quickly as possible, and this includes returning to a familiar work environment. Family, friends, and colleagues must be prepared to hear long and sometimes repetitive anecdotes about the experience. (This is true not only of hostage and kidnap situations, but of almost any traumatic experience a victim has been through. Many war veterans, for example, have trouble putting it behind them.) These stories have a cathartic value, and should be encouraged. Writing and speaking on the subject (if there is sufficient interest in the incident) also provides an outlet for victims who are still trying to bring the experience into some kind of perspective.

Specific reactions over the longer run will vary, but many former hostages report recurrent nightmares, insomnia, phobias, night sweats, and stress-related physical symptoms such as backache. After prolonged captivity, many victims have shown less resistance to illness (even after apparent physical health was fully restored), and a greater tendency toward accidents. This is less likely to be the case when the incident has not been especially prolonged, but victims of incidents lasting as little as three days have been known to report symptoms lasting for several years. Professional counseling is a good idea, along with periodic medical checkups, and a healthy dose of patience and understanding on the part of the victim's employers and colleagues.

Divorce and work-related difficulties are also, unfortunately, sometimes among the longer-term effects of a prolonged traumatic experience. These often grow out of the assumption on the part of the victim, as well as those around him or her, that he or she is completely over the experience just because the more visible manifestations have disappeared. As one former Vietnam prisoner of war told us, "My wife and I got through the hard times, but the good times ruined us." It is impossible to say very much about causes and effects in these cases, because some of these marriages and jobs would have ended in any event, but it is necessary that those trying to help victims readjust be aware that deep-seated reactions may persist even though they are not obvious and the victim denies them.

A related problem is the change that often occurs to the family of a victim while the victim is separated from it. Wives who have never balanced a checkbook develop financial skills and children adjust to having only one parent; in short, the entire familial structure can change during the course of a prolonged incident.

Often, the victim returns to find that his or her role is no longer what it formerly was and that, in fact, the family has proven that it can, if necessary, get by without him or her. It is often impossible—nor is it usually wise—for the family to revert to its former self. This can place severe stress upon all concerned.

The hostage or kidnap experience is fraught with psychological trauma for the victim: guilt at not having properly prepared; a sense that capture was in some way the victim's own fault; feelings of powerlessness, panic, and withdrawal; possibly the Stockholm Syndrome; and all the difficulties of readjustment to normal life. There are no easy answers or treatments, but information and self-awareness are critical. If a potential victim has a fairly clear idea of what to expect, he or she has time to reflect upon it and a better chance of responding appropriately and surviving intact. As we have said so often, proper preparation is the key to effective crisis management, both organizationally and personally.

AFFECTED PARTIES: THE FAMILY

The obvious victim is only part of the story, however. Less visible, but just as important, is the effect of a crisis on the victim's family and friends. There are emotional traumas to be dealt with. There are practical problems: children, finances, and so forth. There is the balance that must be struck between the needs of the family on the one hand (information) and what may be best for the victim on the other (secrecy) and there is one added potential concern— informing a family of the death of a loved one. In short, security briefings, victimology, hostage negotiation, and postcrisis treatment are not enough by themselves. An effective crisis management plan must also take into account the needs of the family as well.

Family needs will vary somewhat, depending on the nature of the crisis. However, one situation that remains fairly constant is notification of death. This will require pretty much the same kind of preparation regardless of whether the particular emergency is an induced catastrophe or a disaster. It is also just about the single most unpleasant duty that ever has to be performed. Nothing can make it easy, but following are a few suggestions for at least keeping it from being any worse than it absolutely has to be.

If at all possible, a family should be notified in person before it can hear about it on the news. The death of a loved one is tragic enough; hearing about it for the first time publicly can be shattering. Notification should be made with as little delay as possible, and this makes it imperative that accurate records be kept on employees and their families and periodically reviewed and updated. Types of information that should be recorded include: address, telephone number, spouse's employment, children's schools, name of doctor, medical history, and dental records. (This last is for accurate identification. Prompt notification, in the case of a fire or accident, may depend upon prompt identification of bodies.) This information should not only be regularly updated, but also kept somewhere and in some form that will be immediately available if the need arises.

In the event of a well-publicized incident, a family should also be notified if nothing has happened that affects it. This is an easy point to overlook, because the natural thing in such a situation is to focus on those who are affected, and to forget about those who are not. But imagine a wife hearing on the news about an explosion or a major fire where her husband works. Worried, she tries to find out if he's all right, but everything is in an uproar and it takes a long time for her to be assured that her husband is not—so far as is known—among the victims. By the time she knows everything is all right, she has spent some very uncomfortable hours. If the situation involves employees and families in different countries, those bad hours can become days.

When, for example, the American embassy in Beirut was bombed in 1983, a team of State Department professionals spent a full day telephoning the next-of-kin of every person connected with that embassy to reassure them that the person about whom they were concerned was unharmed. In some cases, that phone call was the first these people had heard that there had been a bombing, so they hadn't even had a chance to start worrying, but that's all right. The aim is to save people as much worry as possible, and that was accomplished in this case. This underlines the value of up-to-date records, an entry as to whom to call in case of emergency, and phone numbers where that person can be reached.

Insofar as possible, notification should be made by someone with some training in "death/severe injury notification." This is a vital skill, something that can help to soften the blow and aid recovery. It is a good idea for a company or agency to make sure it has one or two people on the payroll who have received this type of training. The person charged with making the notification should be either accompanied or shortly followed by a professional trained in crisis counseling and/or grief therapy. This may be a clergyman, social worker, or similar mental health professional. It should be someone familiar with the needs of families in this kind of situation.

Certain family needs are likely to require attention no matter what the emergency. These must be taken into consideration whether the victim has been killed, injured, kidnapped, or in any other way incapacitated. The following list provides a basis upon which to begin.

1. Financial. Decisions have to be made as to whether an employee's regular salary will be continued at the same level and in the same way. Some method of getting salary or any other sort of payment to the family must be arranged. Insurance payments and death or medical benefits must be provided for and

arranged as expeditiously as possible. Check-cashing and/or credit may have to be arranged. Most of this usually will have to be taken care of very quickly and, often, needy family members will not be in any emotional shape to do much on their own.

2. Everyday needs. During a protracted crisis, or after a death, families may need support in the most basic ways: child care, laundry, meal preparation, shopping, and transportation. Someone should be assigned to check on the family a few times a week to see what assistance might be required. Employers might think about providing a car and driver, babysitting service, or similar services, or at least help to arrange such services as required. The appearance of employer interest in time of crisis can do a great deal for morale.

3. Media. We have mentioned the likelihood of media interest in the family and friends of victims. People who are already trying to deal with the emotional trauma inherent in such a situation do not need intrusive phone calls, badgering by reporters and photographers, and microphones shoved in their faces. Every effort should be made to shield affected parties from such unwanted attention. If the family agrees, someone can be assigned to screen media inquiries.

In a prolonged emergency, this can be more of a problem. Families sometimes feel that not enough is being done for the victim, and they may decide that what is needed is more publicity. This can, in some circumstances, be damaging to the efforts of those trying to save the victim—for example, in hostage or kidnapping situations. Balancing the wishes (and rights) of the family against what is thought to be best for the victim is a delicate matter, and there is no easy answer. Keeping family members fully informed about all that is being done, and counseling them about the likely effects of their talking to the media, may help to ameliorate the problem somewhat.

4. Information. In any sort of ongoing emergency, family and friends of the victim will want to be kept current even if not much is happening. Part of this is a genuine need to know; part of it is the desire for continuous reassurance. The more that can be shared with people in this position, the better. Responses like, "Don't worry, we'll let you know if anything develops," are not usually very satisfying and tend if anything to make matters worse. We recommend that one member of the Crisis Action Team be designated to keep in touch with victims' families throughout an incident, not only to share such information as is available, but also to demonstrate institutional interest and to help keep up morale.

5. Long-term support. This may take a number of different forms, including the need for continuing psychological counseling, financial help, and, possibly, career counseling. The important point is that a family's need for help may not end simply with the termination of the emergency. A major disaster or induced catastrophe, even if it appears to have been resolved fairly quickly, can leave scars in many ways for a long time. It is important to remember

that some long-term follow-up will be necessary, over and above the kinds of help we have been discussing.

INVISIBLE VICTIMS: THE CRISIS ACTION TEAM

The stresses and strains on the victim and those close to him or her are by far the worst, but they are not the entire story. The people who serve on the Crisis Action Team, the ones who may have to make the life-and-death decisions and organize the entire effort, the ones who are under constant pressure from so many different sources, are also victims. They are under stress for the duration of an incident, and their decisions—and mistakes—are made in the full glare of publicity and are subject to the most intense postincident scrutiny. If crisis workers are to perform effectively, they must be fully aware, going in, of what awaits them. Only if they know what kinds of stress they can expect, and how to handle it, can they preserve their own wellbeing and contribute usefully to the successful resolution of an incident. Chapter 9 details the usefulness of simulations in this regard. Here, we wish to point out some of the often-unrecognized effects of crisis upon those charged with responding to it.

The Crisis. No one can be exposed to a traumatic event, however distantly, without being affected by it. This is especially true when a crisis worker must deal with the grim details for hours or days. Death, injury, physical destruction, and human suffering—all of which may be present in any given situation—have a traumatic effect on the people who have to deal with them, however remotely. Rescue workers are particularly susceptible, but stress is also great on the people who have to make the necessary decisions regarding such things as evacuations, hostage negotiations, and notification of victims' families.

A second source of stress is the feeling of frustration as a crisis goes on, giving rise to feelings of impotence and meaninglessness. Crisis management is supposed to mean solving problems and saving lives—that's why people serve on crisis action teams in the first place. But not every incident is going to have a successful resolution and not every decision is going to be right. As crisis workers meet with delays and disappointments, and as their earlier decisions may be called into question, they are likely to experience a good deal of stress, which in turn can negatively affect their performance throughout the rest of the emergency.

Media coverage can also add to the frustration. First, media interest can make crisis workers feel that their every move must be letter-perfect. This merely increases pressure and makes job performance that much more difficult. The media sometimes will be highly critical of how the job is being done, or imply that not enough is being done or resent that more information is not made available to the public. While the media generally try to be fair, their very presence can have a deleterious effect on an already sensitive crisis team, and every implied criticism can aggravate that sensitivity. (This is, by the way, another good reason for funneling media access to the designated public affairs person on the team.)

The Job. The work itself, quite apart from the emergency, brings with it its own kinds of pressure. A member of a crisis action team may find himself or herself performing functions with which he or she is not completely familiar and assuming levels of responsibility beyond that to which he or she is accustomed. No matter how much one prepares for an emergency, its onset is always something of a surprise, and it is impossible to anticipate everything. Crisis workers will find themselves called upon to do things they have not previously had to do in their normal jobs. As the emergency unfolds, they may also have to back each other up, taking on functions for which they have not even had much preparation or briefing. (Chapter 9 discusses these points.) As responsibilities increase, and the nature and volume of the work changes, stress can reach very high levels.

Furthermore, the work environment and schedule become extremely demanding. An ongoing crisis may require around-the-clock monitoring, frequently causing operations to be understaffed. Crisis workers may find themselves putting in long hours, at odd times, with insufficient rest. Workspace may be crowded or uncomfortable or, under some circumstances, even dangerous. Fatigue is likely, just at a time when clear thinking is critical.

The Organization. Given the hours and intensity of work a crisis requires, the members of the Crisis Action Team develop an intimate relationship, not only with each other, but also with the organization for which they work. The immediate situation tends to dwarf other considerations, and workers become caught up with the job at hand. Their self-esteem is to a large extent dependent on how well the crisis is being managed, at least for the duration of the incident. Consequently, failures of the organization—lack of adequate supplies, breakdowns in communication, seemingly unnecessary delays—are magnified, and every such failure adds to the burden of stress already being carried by the individual worker. Much of this is avoidable through good planning, but there will be lapses and human errors. In the midst of an emergency, with lives in the balance, these problems may assume disproportionate dimensions for members of the team.

Because there is often not a lot of leeway in a crisis, and sound, reasonable decisions may have to be arrived at very quickly, it is vital that Crisis Action Team members be aware of the pressures under which they are working and be prepared to do something about them. When an individual's stress level is too high and his or her judgment is starting to be affected, he or she needs a break. Unfortunately, a person hard at work in the middle of a crisis is just about the worst judge of his or her own stress level. Deeply involved in the job, with the adrenaline pumping away, most workers will insist that they are all right. It is important that crisis workers be familiar with the signs of stress, and that supervisors carefully monitor these. All of the preparations and supplies in the world are useless if team members are too physically and mentally exhausted to make rational decisions.

The most obvious symptoms of stress are physical: high blood pressure, headaches, nervousness, fatigue, nausea, or faintness. Even the affected team member should be able to recognize these. Harder to recognize in oneself, but at least as important are: disorientation, inability to concentrate, diminished comprehension, limited attention span, memory difficulties, and, worst of all, loss of objectivity. There may also be irritability,[7] restlessness, unfocused anger, depression, and detachment. (This can be particularly trying for the family members of crisis action team members. The nature of a crisis is such that its effects, the pattern of victimization, extend all the way to the spouses and children of the people who are working to limit the damage, even though they may be many miles from the incident itself.)

A good crisis team leader must be ready for the appearance of these symptoms, be able to recognize them, and know what to do about them. Human skills are ultimately the most important resource in crisis management and these skills must be kept sharp. In order to minimize the effects of stress on Crisis Action Team members, and to deal with those problems that do arise, we offer the following suggestions.

1. First and foremost, *team morale is a critical factor.* Workers perform better when they believe that others care about them and that their good work is being appreciated. As far as possible, a Crisis Action Team should be made up of people who can get along together under difficult circumstances. This is the ideal, of course, and may be hard to achieve in the everyday world. But it is a factor that needs attention in both the setting up and the operation of a team.

   The team leader has a special responsibility for keeping up morale. He or she must try to avoid, or minimize, conflicts between team members (which can occur under stressful conditions), smooth over the organizational rough spots, and make sure that individuals' accomplishments, however routine, are noted and appreciated. It sounds like a simple thing, but for that reason it is easily overlooked. Under the intensified emotional pressure of a crisis situation, it can mean the difference between a smoothly functioning operation and a team close to burnout.

2. A schedule of shifts and breaks should be arranged and *adhered to.* The need for this is obvious; what is less obvious is that team members will often find excuses to skip breaks and stay on the job. The work can be exciting, and

people are sometimes afraid they will miss something. (Crisis management is generally episodic in nature. People who have sat through the "nothing" stretches hate to miss out on the excitement.) Also, some workers may feel indispensable, while others may be afraid that taking time off will make it appear that they are less dedicated (or important) than their colleagues.

It is up to the team leader to schedule regular shifts and regular breaks; to see to it that the staff understands that taking breaks will not be seen as a diminution of effort on their part; to monitor, or have someone else monitor, the stress level of team members and to take corrective actions as needed; and, perhaps most difficult of all, to set the example by eating properly, taking scheduled breaks, and adhering to the schedule.

3. As far as possible, work should be planned in advance. Crisis Action Team members should be briefed fully on what they can expect during various types of emergencies, both in terms of the required work and the expected stress. A good idea is to have a list drawn up well in advance of relatively easy (but necessary) jobs to be done during an emergency. When some workers are wearing down under the tension, they can be rotated to these less-demanding jobs until they can recover themselves somewhat. *All personnel should be rotated through these jobs.* Otherwise, being assigned these functions will simply appear to be a demotion from the "real" work, and team members will resent—or resist—being given them. The idea is to have these jobs done on a rotating basis, while the team leader has them available for assignment to team members who are clearly in need of less-stressful work for a while.

4. Discussion sessions should be programmed for the ends of shifts. People need to share information and ideas, to feel part of the team, to compare notes on how the situation is going, and even to gripe among themselves about the things that seem wrong. Such exchanges are useful for the correction of small problems before they become big ones, the improvements of communication and morale, and the release of tension that is so vital to the effective management of stress.

5. Health concerns are vital. Ideally, a mental health professional should be available, but if this is not possible, a team member should be assigned to monitor such things as eating, exercise, and rest breaks for the rest of the team. Special attention should be paid to the following:

   • *Food.* Crisis team members should not skip meals. It is easy to get involved with the work and to forget to eat, or to substitute junk food snacks (some employees seem to take a perverse pride in doing so), but it is not a good idea. Lack of proper nutrition in a crisis—especially an extended one—can adversely affect a person's judgment. It also needlessly increases stress levels. Besides eating balanced meals at regular intervals, team members should have appropriate snacks available while they are working: fruits, vegetables, nuts, and high-protein foods like granola bars, as well as quantities of coffee, tea, milk, fruit juices, and mineral water.

- Exercise. The demands of crisis management make it imperative that team members be in good physical shape. Regular exercise is important in reducing stress, increasing stamina, and improving circulation (important to mental alertness). It is a good idea to designate an exercise area, close to the Crisis Management Center, and to provide a few things like jump ropes and hand weights. Even in a relatively confined space, isometrics and calisthenics are worthwhile.

- Amenities. These include adequate toilet facilities, basic medications like aspirin and antacids, drinking water, and a rest area provided with pillows, blankets, and some reading material or a television set.

Finally, like the direct victims of an incident, the team members must be prepared for a certain amount of post-traumatic stress symptoms. Most common is the inability to let down, the continuation of the strong emotional grip of the situation they have just been through. Many people are also deeply affected by what they have seen and heard—especially those who have had to share the families' grief. Crisis team members cannot just be told "well done" at the end of the emergency and then be expected to return to their workaday jobs with no transition. They must be given a chance to talk out their experiences and to vent their emotions. We recommend a session or two in which the team can share their triumph (or failure, if that's the way it came out), talk about their feelings, and make plans for improving their institution's approach to crisis management. This has the highly therapeutic effect of helping team members to let go gradually, and it also has the added advantage of allowing the group to plan for the next crisis while the lessons of the one just past are still fresh in their minds. As is the case with every crisis, *planning* does the most to ensure a favorable result.

VICTIMS, FAMILIES AND STAFF IN CRISES: A CHECKLIST

✔ Make certain that all employees have been given a security briefing that will acquaint them with threat levels and recommended precautions.

✔ Establish a program to counsel all employees regarding the importance of arranging such things as inventories, wills, insurance, and so on, and encourage them to discuss this with other members of their families.

✔ Provide potential kidnap/hostage victims with training in survival and rapport-building techniques.

✔ Make arrangements to assist victims' families during and after the emergency.

✔ Ensure that facilities have been provided for victims once the immediate crisis is over.

✔ Ensure that arrangements have been made for the Crisis Action Team members after the incident has been resolved and that facilities are available for them to relax during the emergency.

✔ Acquaint employees and families with the symptoms of stress.

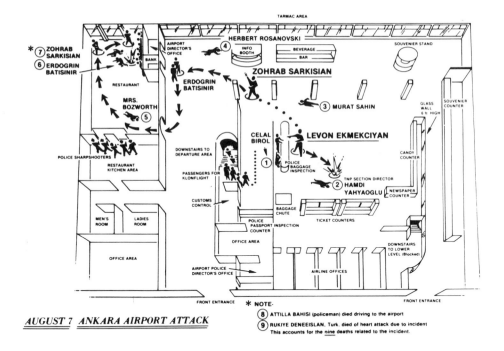

TARMAC AREA

HERBERT ROSANOVSKI

* (7) ZOHRAB SARKISIAN
(6) ERDOGRIN BATISINIR

AIRPORT DIRECTOR'S OFFICE

(4) INFO BOOTH

BEVERAGE BAR

SOUVENIR STAND

BANK

RESTAURANT

ERDOGRIN BATISINIR

ZOHRAB SARKISIAN

GLASS WALL 6 ft HIGH

SOUVENIER COUNTER

MRS. BOZWORTH (5)

(3) MURAT SAHIN

CANDY COUNTER

POLICE SHARPSHOOTERS

RESTAURANT KITCHEN AREA

DOWNSTAIRS TO DEPARTURE AREA

PASSENGERS FOR KLONFLIGHT

CELAL BIROL

(1)

LEVON EKMEKCIYAN

POLICE BAGGAGE INSPECTION

(2) HAMDI YAHYAOGLU

TNP SECTION DIRECTOR

NEWSPAPER COUNTER

CUSTOMS CONTROL

BAGGAGE CHUTE

TICKET COUNTERS

MEN'S ROOM

LADIES ROOM

POLICE PASSPORT INSPECTION COUNTER

OFFICE AREA

OFFICE AREA

AIRPORT POLICE DIRECTOR'S OFFICE

AIRLINE OFFICES

DOWNSTAIRS TO LOWER LEVEL (Blocked)

FRONT ENTRANCE

FRONT ENTRANCE

AUGUST 7 ANKARA AIRPORT ATTACK

* NOTE:
(8) ATTILLA BAHISI (policeman) died driving to the airport
(9) RUKIYE DENEEISLAN, Turk, died of heart attack due to incident
This accounts for the *nine* deaths related to the incident.

The flow of events during the August 7, 1982 ASALA attack on Ankara's Esenboga International Airport are shown above. Mrs. Bozworth (number 5), an American citizen, was one of nine people who died as a result of this incident. Below, security personnel are positioned outside the Esenboga Airport restaurant when an ASALA terrorist held fifteen–eighteen people hostage. In all, over 200 policemen from three police sections were involved in the airport attack. (Source: *Threat Analysis Division, Bureau of Diplomatic Security, U.S. Department of State*)

This is one view of the result of the August 7, 1982 ASALA attack at Esenboga International Airport in Ankara, Turkey. (Source: *Turkish Embassy, Washington, D.C.*)

Johnson & Johnson executives, such as Joseph R. Chiesa, participated in extensive interviews with print and broadcast media to give the public the facts about the Tylenol situation. (Source: *Johnson & Johnson, Inc.*)

A view of damage to Whittier, California from an October 1987 earthquake.
(Photo: *copyright Greg Anderson*)

Fire can completely disrupt an organization's activities unless plans exist for recovery, as the U.S. Postal Service demonstrated when its headquarters was severely damaged by a 1984 fire. (Photo: *U.S. Postal Service*)

Crisis Management Centers can be elaborate if circumstances warrant. Here, two views of the situation room at the U.S. Marshals Service Headquarters. (Photos: *U.S. Marshals Service*)

The State Department recently remodeled and updated the equipment and configuration of its Operations Center. (Photos: *U.S. Department of State*)

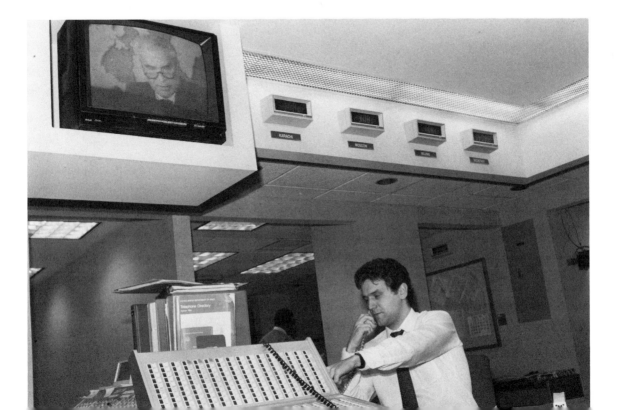

These two pages: **The National Military Command Center at the Pentagon is the military nerve center in time of crisis.** (Photos: *Robert D. Ward and Helene Stikkel, U.S. Department of Defense*)

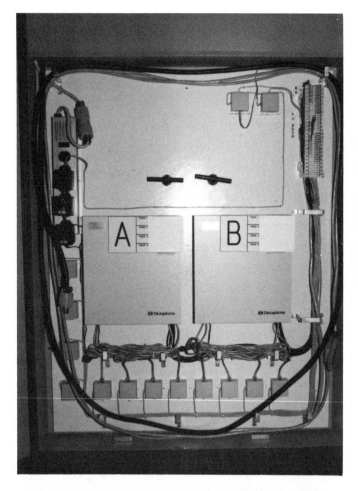

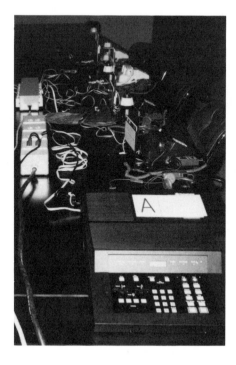

Top: **Simulations are an integral part of military training.** (Photo: U.S. Department of Defense) *Bottom:* **Simulations need not be elaborate nor do they require extensive facilities. This control team is conducting a simulation at a U.S. embassy.** (Photo: *Mayer Nudell*)

Opposite page: **Some views of how a major U.S. corporation can rapidly turn a conference room into a crisis management center. Note how a large quantity of equipment can be stored aesthetically in a small space. The cabinet's dimensions are 77"h × 36"w × 33"d. It contains eight telephones (five direct, three via switchboard); two recorders, each capable of handling four phones at once; four digital and one world clocks; one am/fm radio and one shortwave receiver; tools and keys for the building; access cards for the building; and backup phones. All the equipment is marked and can be ready for use within forty-five minutes.** (Photos: *Mayer Nudell*)

The Office of Foreign Disaster Assistance conducts simulations of disaster relief operations in its own task force room within the State Department. (Photo: *U.S. Office of Foreign Disaster Assistance*)

Simulations are an effective way for tactical units to train personnel. Here the Special Operations Group of the U.S. Marshals Service conducts an exercise. (Photo: *U.S. Marshals Service*)

SIMULATIONS: PUTTING YOUR CRISIS ACTION PLAN TO THE TEST

9

In July 1979, concerned about the immediate aftermath of the coming Sandinista victory, the State Department ordered the withdrawal of all but a handful of the staff of our embassy in Managua. Before the departure of the bulk of the staff and the military specialists deployed on temporary duty, one of the authors (then assigned to the embassy) noted two anomalies in the plan developed for the possibility that the embassy would be attacked and that a rescue mission might be required. According to the plan, he was to take charge of the team detailed to destroy documents and, at the same time, single-handedly clear the landing zone of trees and other obstructions for the rescue helicopter. In addition to the difficulty of being in two places at once, the chain saw he was given to cut the trees required two people to operate it because of a malfunction. Fortunately, no attack occurred.

Emergency planners have long known that effective planning requires considerable foresight and does not occur by accident. Treated with the necessary deliberation and supported by the proper types and quantities of resources, an

This chapter first appeared as "Simulating Crises: The Emergency Manager's Planning Tool," *Clandestine Tactics and Technology*, copyright 1987 by Mayer Nudell.

emergency plan can be the difference between successful coping and total disaster. However, creating the plan is only half of the process. No plan, regardless of its elaborateness and apparent comprehensiveness, should be expected to work properly if it has not been tested before its emergency use.

This sort of situation occurs with frightening regularity in all plans and has little to do with the competence of the planners. Murphy's Law is as much a part of coping with emergencies as it is a factor in daily life. Frequently, it is the little thing—the detail that comes from training and experience and is not considered suitable for codification in the plan itself—that can spell the difference between success and failure in an emergency. The evaluation of an emergency plan and the preparation of those who will react to a crisis should not be left to chance. Real incidents require real and often irrevocable decision-making that involves lives. Short of a real emergency, simulation is the only method of providing nonthreatening situations in which policies, procedures, and capabilities can be evaluated.

The focus of a crisis situation is on the leadership and staff of the emergency teams. Simulations allow the teams to use and assess procedures and plans and to factor into the equation whatever specialized knowledge and/or experience team members might have. This sharing of knowledge and experience is one of the most valuable aspects of the simulation because it provides training and plan evaluation at the same time.

The experience gained and the mistakes made in simulations become the basis for objective lessons and evaluations that can be factored into the planning process. Changes in objective factors and unanticipated variations can be accommodated in a simulation, without the permanent consequences of failure. Periodic exercise of an emergency plan is an essential part of any dynamic planning process.

SIMULATION OBJECTIVES

Crisis simulations, as with any other types of training, are intended to provide opportunities to improve existing skills and to teach new ones. The major difference between crisis management training and other types is that emergencies require rapid decision-making and immediate staff work. The simulation can be tailored in any way desired, from a superficial, across-the-board touching upon all elements of the emergency plan, to a specific, in-depth focusing upon one particular kind of crisis.

There are many reasons to exercise an emergency plan. Simulations allow for practice of routine and extraordinary procedures. They allow participants to work with each other in a crisis atmosphere in which unfamiliar events and stresses occur. Extraorganizational relationships can be evaluated in this atmosphere as well. Informational needs, communications requirements, and lead times for performing tasks can be evaluated. Administrative requirements can be reviewed. Differences between governmental and corporate policies, as well as competing goals and objectives of different organizations and agencies, will be revealed and can be factored into emergency planning. Finally, the impact of media, families, and normal organizational operations can be reviewed to ensure that contingency planning has fully and accurately taken account of them.

Achieving these objectives requires some preconditions. First, participants should be performing the same functions during the simulation that they would be in a real emergency. Some role-playing can enhance the training, but too great a difference between the role played and a real crisis can be counterproductive. The involvement of principals in simulations is a key factor in their effectiveness. Second, participants must be willing to suspend their disbelief and treat the simulation as if it were the real thing. If players do not "get into their roles," the simulation will become a mere game and the players will neither act as they would in the real world nor gain meaningful feedback regarding crisis management skills. Third, controller participants should be familiar with the standard operating procedures and the chain of command of the organization. This is especially important for interagency or other multiactor simulations. Fourth, and perhaps most importantly, all participants must be willing to use the simulation as an opportunity to critically examine their organization's procedures and to consider alternatives to them in the light of the situation posited. Such alternatives might include the team's operating style, the organization's reporting requirements, and even the physical layout of the area in which the emergency team operates during the crisis.

SETTING THE STAGE

Before examining the preconditions for a successful simulation in more detail, we must devote a few moments to considering how to put the participants into the proper frame of mind for the simulation. All participants should recognize the value of contingency planning and fully cooperate in the simulation. This is not always the case; hence the importance of setting the stage for the exercise. (Readers seeking help or guidance in this or any other facet of simulations may wish to refer to Appendix B, which contains a listing that includes a number of companies and individuals offering this service, and Appendix D, which provides more information about staging simulations.)

This background piece is a crucial part of the exercise, because it provides the rationale for the simulation. If the exercise is to occur in a simulated future, the background piece accounts for the intervening time and explains how conditions evolved from those in fact to those at the start of the exercise. If the simulation is intended to exercise elements of an emergency plan for a contingency that is currently unlikely, the background piece allows the exercise controllers to set a plausible stage for the required events.

Not all simulations require a background piece. For example, if the exercise simulates a terrorist attack in a country with a history of such attacks, events will proceed from a starting point that is current and known to all, and no background explanations or rationales are required. The same could be true in an exercise being held shortly before a major international event such as the Olympics or a conference. The important things to remember about background pieces are that they make credible the events simulated by setting the stage for hypothetical political, military, social, economic, financial, law enforcement, or other conditions that lead to the simulated crisis or emergency.

Because of the importance of the background piece, it is important that it be as accurate and in-depth as is possible. Even when it is projected into the future (or is explaining a wholly fictitious situation), it must be based on current realities in order to provide a credible transition to the situation at the start of the simulation (STARTEX). Unless the emergency simulated is exclusively an act of God, the background piece documents in a logically acceptable chronology the deterioration in conditions which is postulated at STARTEX.

PLAYER ROLES

The importance of having participants perform their actual roles during a simulation is often overlooked. Senior officials in government and the private sector are often too busy to devote time to "playing hypothetical games." Contingency planning as a whole is often relegated to the security office and participating in exercises is viewed as a waste of valuable time and resources. Planners and security officers know that nothing is further from the truth.

One of the important differences between how the United States government conducts its simulations and how other governments conduct theirs can be seen in the matter of whether senior governmental civilian officials participate. In the United States, this is rarely the case. In the United Kingdom, for example, Prime Minister Margaret Thatcher has been known to participate in simulated terrorist situations. This willingness of the most senior British official to participate adds immeasurably to the effectiveness of the simulation and, therefore, to the overall value of the contingency plan. A look at the activities of the players during the exercise shows why.

To attain the overall goals of the simulation, players will:

- actively participate in the decision-making and crisis management;
- interact and coordinate with other players, many of whom represent other organizations and interests;
- employ the organization's approved procedures and follow operating guidelines under pressure of events;
- report on and analyze events as they unfold; and
- implement the currently existing contingency plan to respond to events and recommend courses of action to superiors.

The presence of the most senior organizational officials can only enhance this process.

While it is important that players perform their real tasks during the simulation, the exercise does have value as a training vehicle beyond this. For example, a police official could play a hostage to learn something about the pressures hostages are under. Or a mid-level bureaucrat could play his boss, in order to gain some risk-free on-the-job training for a future position. These sorts of cross-training can be valuable. However, a full-dress simulation is not the place for a newspaper reporter to play the police chief or for an intelligence officer to pretend to be a bank president. Role-playing that enhances the benefits and effectiveness of the simulation makes for good training; role-playing for fun is counterproductive and can reduce the simulation's value.

SUSPENSION OF DISBELIEF

Many simulations require the postulation of circumstances very different from those currently being experienced. The State Department's Crisis Management Exercise Program is a good example of this. In this type of exercise, the background piece is of extreme importance, because many of the U.S. embassies at which the exercises are held enjoy tranquil conditions and the types of disasters and other emergencies simulated are quite unlikely there. State's program is intended to accomplish two objectives: (1) provide an opportunity for senior embassy officers to evaluate their Crisis Management Plans and (2) provide training in crisis management for the officers on the Crisis Management Team. Therefore, the background piece projects a fictitious but plausible future situation.

Because Foreign Service officers are intensely preoccupied with the current situation in their country, they often are unable to explore alternative situations that might occur there. This can lead to resistance to the postulated events as "unreal" or "unlikely to occur here anytime soon." The success of a simulation, however, depends on the players' suspension of disbelief and their immersion in the exercise to the point of accepting the artificial environment of the exercise for the limited period of time it takes to stage it. To assist players in making this mental leap, the background piece is carefully tailored to the specific country and its situation. The overall situation in that country is placed in a worldwide context, and events in the United States, and the geographic region are explored in some detail. If properly done, all but the most recalcitrant of players will assume the proper spirit.

Once begun, it is important that the momentum of events be sustained and that implementors be injected into the exercise in as close to a real-life manner as is possible. Telephones, radios, telegrams, face-to-face meetings, memoranda, media and other items should all be used as appropriate, and normal formats, psychological quirks, and so forth should be employed as they would in real life. (Most of these details will be uncovered during the research for the background piece; more can be learned and inserted by discussing the scenario with knowledgeable persons who will not be playing.)

STANDARD OPERATING PROCEDURES

Ideally, each player will be familiar with the standard operating procedures of the organization. Even better, he or she will have reviewed the contingency plan before the exercise and will be conversant with its contents, at least with regard to his or her own role on the emergency team. Normally, at least one of these will be the case. Happily, a byproduct of simulations is to remedy any deficiencies in this regard.

Every organization has standard operating procedures and an approved chain of command for use in routine or extraordinary situations. The routine usually takes care of itself; it is the extraordinary situation that requires precise action. Unlike the normal activities of an organization, a fast-breaking situation may not allow time for complete staff work and for prolonged deliberation. An emergency plan that does not provide a streamlined approach to crisis management is an induced catastrophe of its own.

This is an area in which the controllers have an advantage. They know what is going to happen and they should know what the emergency plan calls for in terms of response. This advantage translates into an opportunity to posit unexpected situations, such as the absence of a key person (who will take over?), the unavailability of a key resource (is there a substitute available?), or the absence of anticipated information sources (does a course of action make sense?). In this atmosphere, planners and players can see if the proposed chain of command or a planned action makes sense in practice. Expected interorganizational coordination and actions can be reviewed and improved.

PLAN REVIEW

The true value of the simulation is its ability to provide an extensive test of an organization's emergency plan. Planning is a dynamic process that includes constant updating and evaluation, along with periodic exercising for training and familiarity. Circumstances change and so do people; what works in one situation or country may no longer be applicable. What appears to be an effective plan may not be so when thoroughly exercised. The final activity in any simulation should be a review of the plan and the organization's procedures, first by the players, then by the controllers.

The players' self-evaluation is extremely important. After all, they are the ones on the firing line and they feel the effects not only of the emergency, but also of the consequences of its resolution. Their perceptions—especially immediately following the simulation—will be based on operational concerns. If the organization is large enough, these operational concerns may be quite different from those of headquarters and this is important for all to understand.

The controllers' evaluation supplements that of the players, if the latter have done a good job in their self-evaluation. The controllers, organizational outsiders to enable them to retain complete objectivity, should not hand out grades or be overly critical. After all, the purpose of the simulation is to learn in a risk-free environment and most errors are likely to have resulted from inexperience or a perspective different from that of the controllers.

Both evaluations cover essentially the same ground. Following are some examples of the areas these evaluations should cover, from planning and training perspectives.

- Was the plan workable overall?
- What problems were identified in the exercise?
- Were the plan's procedures followed?
- How quickly was the emergency team able to organize and begin to function effectively?
- Were the facilities and resources provided to the emergency team adequate? How can they be improved?
- Was information shared effectively and fully within the emergency team?
- Were the players familiar with their organization's operating procedures and chain of command? Were they familiar with those of other involved organizations?
- Was there effective liaison with external actors such as governmental officials, families, and media?

- Were routine matters referred to appropriate personnel or did the emergency team allow itself to be distracted by them?
- Was information reported on an accurate and timely basis? Were analyses prepared as appropriate? Were the proper people and organizations kept informed?
- Were supplies adequate?
- Were public affairs handled effectively? Was a rumor control established?
- Did personality factors impede effective crisis management?

SIMULATION METHODOLOGY

The basic techniques for accomplishing a simulation are straightforward. The people who prepare the exercise should also act as controllers during it, augmented by some knowledgeable personnel from the facility or organization being exercised. While the control team will have much to do during the exercise, it is important that controllers be as few as possible and as invisible as possible in order maintain the realistic atmosphere and to avoid adversely affecting free play. A basic controller team consists of a chief controller, a senior controller, an administrative controller, and specialist controllers.

The chief controller provides the overall guidance to the control team and is the principal liaison with the players. He or she will provide the inbriefing and the final evaluation. The senior controller takes the lead in the actual preparation of the background piece and scenario, along with the implementors, and it is his or her job to oversee the control team during the exercise to ensure that schedules are kept, roles are played properly and implementors modified as required. He or she also will supervise the considerable amount of free play that will occur during the simulation.

An administrative controller is responsible for recording events as they occur during the exercise and for injecting implementors as directed by the schedule or the senior controller. One or more specialist controllers are added to the team as required to deal with the simulation of local variables, operational details, and other technical matters in which they are proficient.

In the early stages of the preparation of the exercise, the chief controller and senior controller determine the specific learning objectives and focus of the exercise and prepare the appropriate background piece and implementors. The manner of implementor injection is determined, as is the schedule of injections. It is rare that an entire exercise can be pre-scripted, so the senior controller must be prepared to engage in free play with the players as events unfold. It is the free play that gives the simulation much of its realism and the senior controller, assisted by the specialist controllers, must be prepared to encourage and respond to a significant amount of it. Unless there is a "book solution" to the exercise, this free play is essential to a successful simulation. If the scenario is too fixed or complicated, it will detract from the free play.

An effective simulation cannot be completely prepared away from the scene of the exercise. Shortly before STARTEX, the control team should inspect the exercise site and fine tune the implementors to physical, political, or other local conditions. For example, street names, persons, etc. should all be verified.

Before STARTEX, the chief controller should give all players a briefing on the philosophy and rules of the simulation. He or she should stress the "no fault" nature of the exercise and the fact that players can make no assumptions regarding information available to them, what developments have or have not occurred, or whether actions they have directed others to take have in fact been taken. Unlike in the real world, the players will have no contact except for the controllers. The role of controllers in this regard is of vital importance. Each controller must be prepared to play a multitude of roles, for the control team will simulate the entire world apart from the players; that is, everyone from foreign governments to the motor pool drivers and from nonplaying staff members to the media and ordinary citizens. While players are free to determine their staffing requirements and to take any actions they wish, all loops must be closed via the controllers. This inbrief is the time when the background piece is distributed to players for their review before STARTEX.

During the conduct of the exercise, the chief controller should spend most of his or her time with the players to observe their actions and to correlate them with communications received by the controllers from the players. In this way, each side's thought processes and actions can be evaluated after the exercise. The final implementor of the exercise should be one that promotes the self-evaluation discussed earlier. Following the self-evaluation, which should be attended by the chief and senior controllers, a meeting of all players and controllers should review the entire exercise and the chief controller should present the controllers' evaluation of the simulation. Readers desiring more detail concerning the preparation and staging of a simulation can refer to Appendix D, where we provide a step-by-step guide.

CONCLUSION

In today's world, the job of the emergency planner is increasingly difficult. As figure 9–1 depicts, the planning process is a dynamic, continuous one. Whether the plan is for acts of terrorism, disasters, or a sporting event, the interrelationships between organizations and factors is increasingly complex. No responsible planner should be denied the tool that enables him to tie it all together. The small cost in time and resources devoted to an exercise of any contingency plan will more than repay itself should the plan be needed.

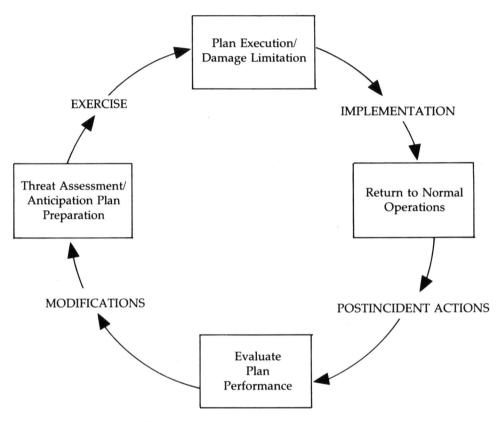

Figure 9–1. The Planning Process

SIMULATIONS: CHECKLIST

- ✔ Develop your comprehensive emergency plan as fully as possible.

- ✔ Identify the sort of exercise you want and determine how much of the plan you want to evaluate.

- ✔ Identify which of your personnel are required to act as players.

- ✔ Arrange for experienced controllers.

- ✔ Arrange for the necessary assistance the controllers will require to prepare and conduct the exercise.

- ✔ Identify where the simulation take place.

- ✔ Decide how long the exercise will last.

- ✔ Decide if the simulation will be carried out in real time or compressed time.

- ✔ Arrange for an immediate evaluation of the exercise after it concludes.

- ✔ Arrange for an in-depth review shortly after the simulation.

RETURNING TO NORMAL: THE DEBRIEFING PROCESS

10

Late on the night of October 15, 1984, a smoke detector activated an alarm light in the Security Force Control Center of the National Post Office Headquarters in Washington, D.C. An apparent short circuit in a computer system had caused a fire to break out on the ninth floor. The fire was detected quickly and firefighting units began arriving within ten minutes of the first alert, but it was already almost too late. In the next eighty minutes the fire would rage through the building, requiring more than 270 fire personnel, forty-five fire engines, thirteen aerial trucks, and thirty-one other types of vehicles before it could be brought under control.

The damage was staggering. Copper wire, which melts at approximately two thousand degrees, melted throughout the electrical system. Walls collapsed, layers of cement broke apart, and metal reinforcing bars melted down. Thousands of gallons of water poured through the building when a three-inch water pipe broke apart on the fifth floor. Water poured down all the way to the lobby, jetting from electrical outlets and streaming from the seams of marble columns and slabs. The flood caused a transformer on one of the lower floors to explode, setting off another *fire. Floors and ceilings collapsed. Almost three thousand employees were displaced by the fire and estimates of the total damage ranged from $15 million to $25 million.*

The cleanup task was also staggering. Nearly every exposed surface in the building suffered fire damage. File cabinets, bookcases, and the insides of desk drawers all had to be cleaned. Walls had to be rebuilt, electrical equipment had to be repaired, rugs and upholstery needed hours and hours of work. Typewriters were cleaned with cotton swabs, computers were disassembled and put back together again, and computer programs and information stored on disks had to be rehabilitated. Over thirteen hundred cleanup workers were employed. And there was still the investigation to determine the cause of the fire.

While the evidence was not conclusive, an electrical short circuit was considered most likely. The Postal Service was actually rather lucky. No one was killed, injuries were minimal (a few firefighters were treated for smoke inhalation; none required hospitalization), and mail service was not disrupted. Even so, the costs in money and time were huge. It would be a full year before all of the departments housed in the headquarters building (which also housed the headquarters of the Public Broadcasting Corporation) would be able to operate again under normal conditions.

Most of crisis management has to do with preparation for a possible incident or operations during an actual one. There is another, equally important element, however, that can begin before the emergency ends and continues after it ends. Some of this is straightforward and self-evident: supplies have to be replenished; equipment has to be relocated; resources have to be reallocated for other, non-emergency functions; and personnel have to be moved back into their normal positions within the organization. Some has to do with treatment of victims after rescue, a subject already touched upon in chapter 8. And some has to do with debriefing and evaluation immediately after the incident. In many ways, this is the most important part. *Remember: The end of every crisis is the beginning of your preparation for the next one.* Nothing is of more value to your future planning than the lessons you learned the hard way in the past.

Not much needs to be said on the first point. All of the things we mentioned earlier as being necessary for the effective operation of a crisis center—snacks, medical supplies, typewriters, and so forth—are going to be necessary again. It is a simple point, but easy to overlook in the euphoria of a successful resolution (or, unfortunately, in the disappointment of an unsuccessful ending). The things that were necessary before will be necessary again, and the time to replace them is right away. It will be of no use during the next emergency to be able to say that you used to have the right supplies, but used them up last time. Also, the immediacy of the experience is helpful in determining your real needs, as opposed to the general checklist we provided earlier. Only through experience will you know just which items were most handy, and which turned out to be less so. When you have that knowledge, act on it; you will be that much readier for the next crisis.

This handbook is intended to provide you with a managerial overview of crisis management and emergency preparations; it is a people book. For this reason, we concentrate on the organizational aspects of our subject and not on the fine points, which you must provide to tailor your preparations and actions for your own circumstances. In keeping with this approach, we have already discussed some of the effects of postincident traumatic stress on both victims and rescue workers (of which crisis managers are a type), and the problems of readjustment after a crisis. There are a few points worth adding here, as we look at the overall process of getting back to normal.

GENERAL OBSERVATIONS

MEDIA STATEMENTS

The resolution of an incident is the focus of the greatest level of media interest— greater even than that at the onset of the emergency. As stated at some length earlier, the media are looking for a good story, and victims' statements can provide just the kind of controversy or revelation to make a story that much juicier. The victim is not likely to be in any shape to objectively weigh all the considerations surrounding the emergency. Deliverance can be as emotionally draining as the original threat itself.

Victims of an induced catastrophe or a disaster often have gone immediately to the press (which was actively seeking their comments, preferably in quotable form) and said things they later regretted. It is not at all uncommon for people to feel that not enough was done to aid them, or that they weren't properly warned, or that their family wasn't properly cared for. Some of these criticisms may be valid, but the time and place for their expression should not be in public when emotions are running highest. Such statements serve only to embarrass the speaker (when he or she finally calms down), annoy and demoralize the members of the Crisis Action Team, and generally make the organization look bad. As far as possible, victims should say nothing to the press beyond how happy they are to have come through the situation. Weightier impressions should be saved for a later time.

EMOTIONAL REACTIONS (VICTIMS)

People who have been through a life-threatening experience or a period of captivity often tend to show similar stress effects afterward. We have mentioned some of these already, but it may be useful to summarize them here.

Self-criticism. Victims often blame themselves for not having avoided the danger in the first place, for not having been properly prepared for it, or for not having handled it better when it did happen.

Criticism of others. Some victims are certain at first that not enough was done to help them, or that it could have been done better or faster. This is particularly true at the end of hostage/barricade or kidnapping situations, where the Stockholm Syndrome is operative.

Guilt. Some victims are beset by a lingering feeling that the incident was somehow their own fault. It is not rational, but emotions often are not, and it is something with which you must be prepared to deal.

Discomfort around others. People who have just been through a traumatic experience have a tremendous need to talk about it, but they may feel that someone who did not share the experience can't possibly understand anything about it. Others can only appreciate a former victim's experiences intellectually, not intuitively, and they may have difficulty giving the victim the kind of response and support that he or she requires. The need to explain, and the frustration of not feeling understood, can combine to make a former victim very tense in the company of others.

Physical symptoms. These may include insomnia, loss of appetite, depression, lower back pain, irritability, and sexual dysfunction, among others. Some of these, particularly sexual problems, can be very difficult for the individual to discuss or even accept.

Most of these residual feelings and symptoms will fade with time. The important thing is for the victim to understand that these are very normal reactions and that they are in no way unique. If the victim can understand that they are also temporary, he or she can get back to work and start returning to normal. Where problems persist, a competent counselor may be helpful. Rarely are any of these problems long-term, however, and it is important that the victim get them in perspective as quickly as possible.

EMOTIONAL REACTIONS (CRISIS ACTION TEAM MEMBERS)

We touched on some of these in an earlier chapter, so we will simply recap here. The important point to remember is that crisis team members can be victims too, and their emotions must also be dealt with in a timely and effective manner.

Difficulty in letting go. A crisis is a very intense experience. It is almost always more interesting than the usual work that most of us do on a day-to-day basis. It often is hard for a crisis team member to give up the ''rush'' of crisis management to go back to the "real" world, and to give up the status attached to that highly specialized and exciting kind of work.

Doubt and self-blame. In even the best of crisis management operations, there will be mistakes and failures. A good crisis action team will by definition be made up of highly motivated people with very high standards of performance. At the end of an emergency (and often during one as well) such individuals will feel the full weight of every error and missed opportunity. They may begin second-guessing their earlier decisions, wondering if they might not have accomplished more through some other alternative. This is especially troublesome if there have been some serious adverse consequences—especially injury or death. Team members may feel the responsibility for some of these things personally, and they may be assailed by doubts.

Blaming others. All sorts of things happen in the intensity of a crisis. Tempers flare, communications falter, messages get lost or garbled, unnecessary delays occur. The purpose of this book, of course, is to help you to minimize such developments, but it is almost impossible to eliminate them entirely. At the end of an incident, all the damage has to be repaired. Team members have to continue working together in their regular environment, and they have to be able to come together again in a future emergency. Doubts and resentments have to be aired and resolved, or personnel changes will have to be made.

Releasing stress. Team members have a lot of stress with which they must deal, but most will find this difficult. They may feel it is unprofessional to show their emotions. Even though they are exposed to a number of extremely upsetting events, and may be stretched near the breaking point physically and emotionally, they may feel obligated to hold it all in. Also, because of the hours they are working, and the confidentiality that usually surrounds what they are doing, they may not have an outlet for the release of pent-up frustration and anxiety.

SOME SPECIFIC SUGGESTIONS

A good crisis management operation can kill several birds with one stone by arranging a series of debriefings soon after resolution of the emergency. This allows for the accomplishment of a number of things: (1) performance can be evaluated and errors recognized and corrected; (2) personnel can express some of their feelings, compare reactions, and so forth, giving them a chance to deal with some of the stress they have been experiencing; and (3) management can take a look at the entire plan, now that it has had its baptism of fire, eliminate any weaknesses, reinforce strengths, and generally be much more prepared for the next incident, should there be one. If the next crisis is resolved more effectively as a result of the lessons learned from the previous one, then some good will have come from an otherwise unpleasant experience.

Details of the debriefings naturally will vary according to circumstances, but here are a few fundamental suggestions.

Do it soon. Everyone will need a little time to let down, of course, so the first twenty-four hours or so should be given over to rest and a feeling of accomplishment. Discussions should be held right after that, however, for two reasons.

First, everything will still be fresh in everyone's mind—not only specific events, but also personal feelings and reactions. People need to share their perceptions, and to do so they must be able to focus on details. Many of these impressions will have been formed while the crisis team members were very busy and possibly quite tired, so they may start to fade soon after the end of the emergency. After, say, a week, team members may not be able to agree on specific events or their chronology. Good contingency planning requires that everyone be able to reflect on the incident accurately. (Incidentally, this is another good argument for keeping accurate and up-to-date logs throughout the emergency.)

Second, if the debriefing is to help crisis team members deal with the emotional reactions, it should be held as soon as possible. People should be given the opportunity to talk things out and to work through their feelings quickly, before longer-term problems can develop. We recommend that, if at all possible, debriefings begin within forty-eight hours of the emergency's resolution.

Keep it confidential. Effective stress management requires that people be able to talk candidly. Fear of reprisal not only is unhelpful but also may actually increase feelings of stress. The purpose of debriefings is to help people to feel better, not to add to their burden. Therefore, team members must feel free to express exactly what they feel. People will be dealing with strong emotions: grief, fear, anxiety, even horror if the incident caused massive loss of life. They need the opportunity to deal with these things honestly and to talk them out without having to fear repercussions.

It should be made clear to all participants at the outset that everything they say will be kept strictly confidential. It is best if management is not present during these discussions. Nothing should be allowed to inhibit the free expression of the team members, and nothing should be carried beyond the confines of the meeting room. Not only will this allow for more effective stress management, but it may also lead to suggestions for improved performance that might otherwise never surface.

Separate the functions. Keep in mind that ventilation and evaluation are really quite distinct from each other. Stress management requires that people be allowed to say whatever is on their mind, to express all their feelings, including anger. Effective critique requires calm and rational analysis. The two (or more) sessions should be kept separate—one for stress management, and one to elicit suggestions for improved future performance. Combining the two in one meeting may inhibit both processes.

Keep it fairly small. A debriefing group should be small enough to give everyone a chance to talk. This should also help to encourage the atmosphere of intimacy necessary to get people to express strong emotions and to understand each other's feelings. A large group—more than ten or twelve people—is likely to mean that either a few will dominate the discussion while others say little or nothing, or several members will compete for the floor, accomplishing nothing.

If a large number of people were involved in the emergency response, we suggest breaking them down into functionally similar groups, such as rescue workers, crisis action team members, support personnel, and so forth. (Remember, by the way, that these meetings should not exclude such support personnel as secretaries, drivers, and others. These people have had their own strains to deal with during the crisis, even if they haven't always been as visible as the others. They might also have some good ideas to offer regarding operational improvements.)

The stress management debriefing should be held first. Once everyone has had a chance to say the things they feel need saying, to get it out of their system and start to return to normal, the rational process of procedural review can be undertaken. Some people may be eager to get through the stress business as quickly as possible, in order to get to the more tangible questions of mechanics, but we recommend taking it a little more slowly and doing it right. You'll get much better operational analysis if you tend to emotional needs first.

The stress debriefing should be led by someone with a mental health background. He or she ideally should have some knowledge not only of the effects of stress and post-traumatic stress disorders, but also of at least the general outlines of crisis operations. A familiarity with group dynamics is also a must.[1]

The aim of such a discussion group is to help crisis team members deal with their reactions and avoid any serious long-term psychological effects. Every group will be different, just as every emergency is different, but the essential goals of these debriefings are as follows.

Venting emotions. People have a need to get things said. They need to be encouraged to express their anger, grief, and frustration. This may mean that a lot of silly and unpleasant things get said, and some feathers get temporarily ruffled. Such things are perfectly acceptable. A good group leader can guide the discussion to help get rid of these feelings without any true harm being done, so that the participants get the maximum benefit.

The "fallacy of uniqueness." Emotions in a crisis situation are necessarily intense, and the reactions after the fact can be unsettling. Team members may experience bizarre dreams, peculiar obsessions, mild phobias, and so on. This is perfectly normal, but *the average person may not realize that*. One of the worst things are about such reactions is the feeling the individual often has that he or she is the only one responding this way, that there is something wrong. A proper stress debriefing will give everyone a chance to talk out their symptoms and to recognize and be reassured that their experience is normal and not unique.

Preparation for further possible problems. Along with reassurance, it is a good idea that team members be given some idea of what to expect. Postincident symptoms can last for weeks or months in one form or another and it would hardly be productive to run stress debriefings for that long. Team members should be given information about the kinds of emotional and physical symptoms that might develop, and an idea of the range of normal and abnormal responses. If further emotional reactions develop, they will be better equipped to handle normal responses and readier to seek professional help for anything else.

THE DEBRIEFING FORMAT

Naturally, there will be considerable variation in debriefing techniques, depending upon time and facilities, available personnel, and the nature of the emergency, but all will have to contain the following elements, pretty much in this order.

1. At the beginning, participants should be clearly told the purpose of the meeting. There may be some resistance at first, because many people tend to deny stress, but the debriefing leader should impress upon all participants how normal this sort of exercise is. Above all, *the principle of confidentiality should be emphasized.* The debriefing will not be useful if the participants hold back.

2. The substance of the discussion should be a review of the facts of the incident. People should talk about what role they played in the affair, the hours they worked, the problems they had, and so forth. This should be as detailed as possible. The idea is to bring the experience to life so participants can explore what they (and others) were feeling throughout the crisis. It is hard to lead people into a discussion of their feelings without this preliminary phase.

3. After reviewing the facts, participants should be encouraged to discuss their feelings at the time of the crisis and afterward. This is the time for venting emotions. Team members should be encouraged to see their reactions in the context of their own private lives. Events can have symbolic meanings for the individual that go well beyond superficial appearances. The death of a victim one hardly knew can become psychologically entangled with the earlier death of a loved one. Frustration at not being able to rescue all the victims in an

incident may trigger unresolved emotions about some seemingly unrelated personal crisis. While discussions of this type may not seem on the surface to have that much to do with crisis management, they can be tremendously helpful to the individuals who have to deal with the consequences of an incident. Since most of these same people are the ones who will have to be ready for the next crisis, the investment in stress management and morale will ultimately pay big dividends to the institution that pays attention to these kinds of considerations.

4. The conversation should then be turned to any emotional or physical symptoms that have surfaced since the crisis. Team members should be encouraged to discuss anything unusual in their behavior—trouble sleeping, physical disorders, fits of crying, inability to deal with grief. Having first aired their feelings, they should be ready to understand that these symptoms are normal manifestations of the stress with which they have been dealing. This understanding should help them to cope more effectively with any problems they might be having.

5. Normality is the key. Participants should come out of a stress debriefing session understanding that their reactions are neither unique nor uncommon. They must recognize that there is nothing wrong with them. Once the problems are talked out, and anxieties about stress symptoms are relieved, participants should be well on their way to putting the incident behind them and getting back to their regular jobs and lives.

A few days later, a separate debriefing can be held to discuss mechanics. Procedures can be reviewed and mistakes corrected (always in a nonjudgmental way). We refer you to the earlier chapters of this book, to compare your own experience and performance in a real-world crisis to what we have suggested for your consideration. Ideally, you will have been fully prepared and no mistakes will have been made. As this is rarely the case, the next best is that you will understand exactly why everything did not go according to plan and will be able to make appropriate changes. Every plan, no matter how good, requires periodic updating, and every crisis should leave you stronger and better prepared for the next one.

AFTER THE CRISIS IS OVER: A CHECKLIST

- ✔ Replenish all supplies expended during the emergency and acquire any other items you believe advisable for future situations.

- ✔ Determine what lessons can be drawn in terms of your organization, personnel, and other crisis management requirements, and ensure that these lessons are used to revise and update your plans and procedures.

- ✔ Evaluate the system created to shield victims from the media in the immediate aftermath of the emergency and determine if your organization has provided sufficiently for their needs, including helping them to vent their stress.

- ✔ Establish a schedule for debriefings and obtain any outside assistance you will require for them.

- ✔ Ensure that all the proper people are included in the debriefings.

- ✔ Ensure that the factual information covered during the debriefings will be distributed to the proper people.

- ✔ Ensure that personal and sensitive information covered during the debriefings will remain confidential.

- ✔ Evaluate the effectiveness of your recovery planning.

WORLDWIDE AND U.S. DISASTERS AND INDUCED CATASTROPHES, 1900–1987

APPENDIX A

The listings below illustrate the type of information that can be acquired concerning the history of disasters and induced catastrophes outside the United States and its possessions, as well as domestically. These listings provide a starting point and they include only the total number of disasters, the number of people affected, and the dollar value of the resulting damage (the U.S. table does not include the number of affected people, because of the manner in which records are kept.) The disasters covered include (but are not limited to): accidents, avalanches, temperature extremes, earthquakes, epidemics, floods, fires, storms, landslides, and pestilence. Induced catastrophes are limited to acts of terrorism and the information is not as complete, but similar information can be obtained for other emergencies. Because of gaps in the records, the statistics should be considered as minimums. *Note that regional statistics refer to multicountry events and do not coincide with totals for individual countries within that region.*

Table A–1. Worldwide Disaster Summary, by Region, 1900–April 1987

Region	Number	People affected	Damage ($)
Africa	12	11,285,847	505,000,000
Asia	2	2,500	63,000,000
Caribbean	3	7,200	n.a.
Central America	1	n.a.	n.a.
East Africa	1	n.a.	n.a.
Europe	18	3,072,411	4,000,000
Near East	5	2,642,126	100,000,000
Sahel	1	100,000	n.a.
South America	1	n.a.	n.a.
Western Sahara	1	70,000	n.a.
Western Samoa	4	96,264	32,488,000
Worldwide	3	20,048,958	n.a.

Source: Data excerpted from statistics of the Office of U.S. Foreign Disaster Assistance, Agency for International Development.

n.a.—not available.

Table A–2. Worldwide Disaster Summary, by Country, 1900–April 1987

Country	Number	People affected	Damage ($)
Afghanistan	14	1,592,445	87,200,000
Albania	2	46	n.a.
Algeria	17	1,599,487	5,265,000,000
Angola	4	1,481,126	n.a.
Anguilla	2	5	n.a.
Antigua	4	75,004	1,000,000
Argentina	27	7,064,405	2,368,000,000
Australia	15	101,717	8,399,600
Austria	3	605	n.a.
Azores	2	44,669	n.a.
Bahamas	9	1,881	17,700,000
Bahrain	1	111	n.a.
Bangladesh	104	167,440,093	2,594,579,000
Barbados	2	460	500,000
Belgium	4	1,566	70,000,000
Belize	7	95,069	82,500,000
Benin	10	1,599,084	5,000,000

Table A–2. continued

Country	Number	People affected	Damage ($)
Bermuda	2	n.a.	1,500,000
Bolivia	23	3,805,613	1,392,018,000
Botswana	10	3,593,440	3,050,000
Brazil	62	50,673,199	4,735,711,000
Bulgaria	3	3,034	n.a.
Burkina Faso	20	4,263,941	707,500,000
Burma	33	3,102,678	143,804,000
Burundi	4	616,584	1,000,000
Cambodia	3	20,130	600,000
Cameroon	3	411,039	1,500,000
Canada	10	4,625	n.a.
Canary Islands	3	1,497	n.a.
Cen. Af. Rep.	3	514,850	125,000
Chad	18	10,087,801	83,100,000
Chile	34	9,165,128	4,495,710,000
China (PRC)	76	57,473,904	3,387,200,000
China (Taiwan)	20	165,421	841,322,000
Colombia	35	6,022,210	2,026,800,000
Comoros Islands	6	105,560	23,000,000
Congo	1	6,000	n.a.
Cook Islands	5	2,000	25,000,000
Costa Rica	14	126,557	41,700,000
Cuba	15	876,052	681,000,000
Cyprus	5	275,900	100,000
Czechoslovakia	1	14	n.a.
Denmark	1	n.a.	n.a.
Djibouti	7	544,178	5,500,000
Dominica	3	80,042	49,250,000
Dominican Rep.	13	1,988,945	267,000,000
Ecuador	28	1,908,046	264,904,000
Egypt	8	107,032	14,000,000
El Salvador	13	2,060,736	919,100,000
Fiji	22	893,708	143,107,000
France	19	54,831	66,500,000
Fr. Polynesia	3	10,007	37,000,000
Gambia	10	1,215,700	31,700,000

Table A–2. continued

Country	Number	People affected	Damage ($)
Germany (East)	2	156	n.a.
Germany (West)	8	1,663	87,000,000
Ghana	8	13,273,165	74,800,000
Greece	14	881,601	1,886,600,000
Grenada	2	2,093	n.a.
Guadeloupe	5	115,039	70,000,000
Guatemala	17	5,532,479	1,017,520
Guinea	1	40,275	n.a.
Guinea Bissau	1	n.a.	n.a.
Guyana	5	285,909	3,100,000
Haiti	23	2,742,415	272,009,000
Honduras	15	1,214,409	684,000,000
Hong Kong	13	34,272	18,000,000
Iceland	3	10,413	24,700,000
India	192	859,830,317	5,811,187,000
Indonesia	101	9,190,925	687,278,000
Iran	50	2,640,745	75,000,000
Iraq	4	1,060,052	10,000,000
Ireland	3	515	n.a.
Israel	1	33	n.a.
Italy	39	2,851,589	23,856,100,000
Ivory Coast	1	1,620	n.a.
Jamaica	24	690,517	231,925,000
Japan	89	8,075,416	2,767,900,000
Jordan	5	1,778,186	45,900,000
Kenya	11	1,150,177	11,550,000
Kiribati	2	1,772	n.a.
Korea (South)	36	7,445,749	629,431,000
Laos	12	4,226,261	32,080,000
Lebanon	8	3,736,571	4,436,000,000
Lesotho	4	784,500	1,000,000
Liberia	5	208,979	200,000,000
Libya	1	320	5,000,000
Macao	1	1,414	n.a.
Malagasy Rep.	16	4,805,787	602,970,000
Malawi	4	47,100	700,000

Table A–2. continued

Country	Number	People affected	Damage ($)
Malaysia	13	761,889	79,563,000
Maldive Islands	1	11,477	n.a.
Mali	18	4,914,735	113,500,000
Martinique	6	67,070	71,000,000
Mauritania	14	6,096,012	62,500,000
Mauritius	8	1,012,174	380,650,000
Mexico	57	2,283,945	4,583,800,000
Mongolia	3	271,257	25,000,000
Montserrat	1	n.a.	n.a.
Morocco	13	657,684	35,600,000
Mozambique	23	23,712,831	239,700,000
Nepal	20	5,005,755	266,813,000
Netherlands	1	302,000	300,000,000
New Calendonia	13	16	3,900,000
New Zealand	4	12,351	20,000,000
Nicaragua	19	2,116,231	3,280,437,000
Niger	26	5,420,004	116,700,000
Nigeria	12	5,584,342	1,400,000,000
Niue	3	11,200	1,541,000
Norway	1	123	n.a.
Oman	1	10,000	n.a.
Pakistan	31	21,246,146	1,299,215,000
Panama	14	76,043	92,404,000
Papua New Guinea	15	88,254	14,650,000
Paraguay	7	499,796	85,050,000
Peru	52	7,358,316	1,787,400,000
Philippines	127	33,675,837	1,661,576,000
Poland	5	28,838	55,000,000
Portugal	11	353,695	130,100,000
Réunion	3	23,035	n.a.
Romania	17	1,616,756	2,500,000,000
Rwanda	8	4,044,517	n.a.
Sâo Tome & Prin.	2	93,150	n.a.
Saudi Arabia	4	2,779	220,000
Senegal	18	7,327,513	382,756,000
Seychelle Is.	1	103	900,000

Table A–2. continued

Country	Number	People affected	Damage ($)
Sierra Leone	2	13,353	3,600,000
Solomon Islands	10	209,703	n.a.
Somalia	11	1,206,198	500,000
South Africa	17	2,498,232	1,000,000
Soviet Union	28	32,058,414	2,810,000
Spain	22	737,100	7,996,000
Sri Lanka	26	11,913,507	220,312,000
St. Kitts	2	n.a.	n.a.
St. Lucia	6	83,019	95,745
St. Martin/Saba	2	n.a.	n.a.
St. Vincent	7	46,475	20,800
Sudan	15	13,151,907	26,442,000
Suriname	1	4,600	50,000
Swaziland	2	633,053	54,152,000
Sweden	3	13	170,000,000
Switzerland	10	269	10,000,000
Syria	4	289,253	44,000,000
Tanzania	18	2,316,511	4,200,000
Thailand	18	7,854,087	519,400,000
Tibet	1	n.a.	n.a.
Togo	5	370,465	700,000
Tokelau	3	n.a.	n.a.
Tonga	7	181,212	25,600
Trinidad & Tobago	3	50,039	38,000,000
Tunisia	9	466,639	198,000,000
Turkey	43	1,612,590	443,800,000
Tuvalu	3	706	n.a.
Uganda	10	2,287,104	1,700,000
United Arab Em.	1	112	n.a.
United Kingdom	15	17,766	42,400,000
Uruguay	3	56,619	39,000,000
Vanuatu	13	127,658	66,250,000
Venezuela	10	285,928	54,126,000
Vietnam	30	17,482,661	73,500,000
Wallis & Futuna	3	4,501	n.a.
Yemen (North)	5	2,943,559	2,022,700,000

Table A–2. continued

Country	Number	People affected	Damage ($)
Yemen (South)	4	365,482	32,200,000
Yugoslavia	16	1,093,712	1,468,200,000
Zaire	10	1,196,369	25,200,000
Zambia	7	90,966	200,000
Zimbabwe	5	917	1,000,000

Table A–3. Major Disasters within the United States and Possessions, 1953–July 1987

State	Number	Dollar Value
Alabama	18	$ 233,489,331
Alaska	12	84,557,766
American Samoa	5	13,762,387
Arizona	11	77,091,689
Arkansas	22	27,832,994
California	42	831,586,158
Colorado	11	43,952,662
Connecticut	6	36,727,836
Delaware	2	3,188,001
District of Columbia	0	0
Florida	23	94,860,676
Georgia	14	8,276,904
Guam	3	42,162,485
Hawaii	14	21,166,972
Idaho	14	43,056,232
Illinois	20	75,980,207
Indiana	11	25,554,655
Iowa	17	19,442,648
Kansas	17	27,703,249
Kentucky	21	128,369,578
Louisiana	26	142,090,582
Maine	8	21,313,582
Marshall Islands	1	234,905
Maryland	8	43,632,340
Massachusetts	10	73,681,444
Michigan	16	61,728,933

Table A–3. continued

State	Number	Dollar Value
Micronesia	1	1,453,964
Minnesota	17	51,352,199
Mississippi	19	202,553,082
Missouri	19	78,329,597
Montana	9	25,308,925
Nebraska	16	45,652,935
Nevada	11	9,042,989
New Hampshire	7	10,153,134
New Jersey	11	59,814,549
New Mexico	12	12,862,290
New York	26	233,470,903
North Carolina	14	38,035,667
North Dakota	14	41,671,124
North Marianas	4	21,355,420
Ohio	20	44,409,178
Oklahoma	29	59,287,118
Oregon	9	26,786,236
Pacific Trust Territory	11	27,899,397
Pennsylvania	22	572,774,144
Puerto Rico	9	281,286,491
Rhode Island	4	6,866,398
South Carolina	3	4,144,988
South Dakota	9	31,391,351
Tennessee	15	32,032,396
Texas	46	248,354,631
U.S. Virgin Islands	6	10,324,073
Utah	3	55,428,028
Vermont	6	26,537,181
Virginia	14	102,921,598
Washington	20	68,557,050
West Virginia	20	191,070,467
Wisconsin	13	25,628,720
Wyoming	4	5,928,282
TOTAL	795	$4,834,128,721

Source: Federal Emergency Management Agency. These data reflect only those disasters declared by the president and the amount of money FEMA was authorized to use from the President's Fund.

Table A–4. Terrorist Attacks, by Region, 1980–1986

Region	1980	1981	1982	1983	1984	1985	1986	Total
Latin America	1,566	1,711	1,760	1,857	2,257	1,933	1,702	12,786
Europe	580	454	359	438	539	471	445	3,286
Asia	108	83	67	106	333	326	420	1,443
North America	27	22	31	14	10	10	7	121
Middle East	426	352	294	352	289	171	212	2,096
Sub-Sahara Africa	48	79	42	71	97	99	74	510
TOTAL	2,755	2,701	2,553	2,838	3,525	3,010	2,860	20,182

Source: Risks International Division, Business Risks International. Note that Risks International uses its own definition of a terrorist attack and these statistics may differ considerably from official government figures or those of other sources.

Table A–5. Victims of Terrorist Attacks, 1980–1986

	1980	1981	1982	1983	1984	1985	1986	Total
Killed	4,843	5,611	6,166	10,159	9,614	7,166	5,142	48,701
Injured	3,381	3,014	3,607	3,953	4,009	5,181	5,618	28,763
Total	8,224	8,625	9,773	14,112	13,623	12,347	10,760	77,464
U.S. killed	19	35	9	301	61	54	12	491
U.S. injured	33	76	31	156	144	160	158	758
U.S. total	52	111	40	457	205	214	170	1,249

Source: Risks International Division, Business Risks International.

Table A–6. International Terrorist Incidents, by Location, 1968–August 1987

Country	Number	Country	Number
Afghanistan	44	Belgium	106
Albania	1	Belize	2
Algeria	7	Benin	1
Angola	46	Bermuda	1
Argentina	394	Bolivia	69
Australia	28	Botswana	7
Austria	72	Brazil	52
Bahamas	4	Bulgaria	3
Bahrain	8	Burkina Faso	1
Bangladesh	14	Burma	9
Barbados	5	Burundi	1

Table A–6. continued

Country	Number	Country	Number
Cameroon	1	Guyana	3
Canada	28	Haiti	12
Canary Islands	5	Honduras	60
Central Af. Rep.	6	Hong Kong	2
Chad	14	Hungary	2
Chile	135	Iceland	2
China	2	India	132
Colombia	277	Indonesia	9
Congo Republic	1	Iran	210
Corsica	9	Iraq	66
Costa Rica	43	Ireland	67
Crete	5	Israel	365
Cuba	5	Italy	403
Cyprus	48	Ivory Coast	2
Czechoslovakia	3	Jamaica	10
Denmark	30	Japan	58
Djibouti	7	Jordan	78
Dominica	1	Kampuchea	11
Dominican Republic	38	Kenya	4
East Germany	2	Kuwait	60
Ecuador	41	Laos	12
Egypt	28	Lebanon	747
El Salvador	155	Lesotho	8
Equatorial Guinea	1	Liberia	2
Eritrea	8	Libya	15
Ethiopia	60	Luxembourg	6
Fiji	1	Malaysia	70
France	483	Malta	11
Gabon	2	Martinique	2
Gaza Strip	67	Mauritania	3
Ghana	1	Mexico	105
Greece	323	Morocco	7
Grenada	1	Mozambique	37
Guadeloupe	5	Namibia	3
Guatemala	132	Nepal	3
Guinea	2	Netherlands	162

Table A–6. continued

Country	Number	Country	Number
New Zealand	9	Suriname	1
Nicaragua	43	Swaziland	8
Nigeria	1	Sweden	30
Northern Ireland	19	Switzerland	97
Norway	5	Syria	86
Oman	3	Taiwan	3
Pakistan	229	Tanzania	6
Panama	12	Thailand	22
Papua New Guinea	1	Togo	3
Paraguay	5	Trinidad & Tobago	9
Peru	206	Tunisia	13
Philippines	106	Turkey	295
Poland	3	Uganda	29
Portugal	55	United Arab Emir.	18
Puerto Rico	44	United Kingdom	149
Qatar	8	United States	448
Red Sea	1	Uruguay	39
Romania	5	USSR	7
Saudi Arabia	12	Vatican City	5
Senegal	2	Venezuela	59
Seychelles	1	Vietnam	1
Sierra Leone	2	West Germany	516
Singapore	16	West Bank	401
Somalia	9	Western Sahara	10
South Africa	13	Yemen Arab Republic	19
South Korea	8	Yugoslavia	17
South Yemen	2	Zaire	9
Spain	350	Zambia	11
Sri Lanka	6	Zimbabwe	28
Sudan	29		
		Total Incidents = 9,139	

Source: U.S. Department of State. Note definition of *international* terrorism.

Table A–7. Terrorist Attacks within the United States, 1980–1986

Year	Incidents	Killed	Injured
1980	29	1	19
1981	42	1	4
1982	51	7	26
1983	31	6[a]	4
1984	13	0[b]	0
1985	7	2	10
1986	17	1	19
Totals	190	18	82

Source: Federal Bureau of Investigation.

[a]Two additional deaths resulted from the attempted arrest of Sheriff's Posse Comitatus member Gordon Kahl on June 3, 1983.

[b]One death resulted from the attempted arrest of Aryan Nations member Robert Mathews on December 7, 1984.

RESOURCE LIST FOR CONTINGENCY PLANNERS

APPENDIX B

<hr>

The following list provides planners with starting points for developing information and identifying crisis management assets and resources outside their own organizations. This list is not exhaustive; rather, we have indicated herein a number of sources we *know* to be reputable from our own experience. This doesn't mean other sources should not be used where appropriate, only that we have no firsthand knowledge of them. This list does *not* constitute any endorsement of particular companies. *Please note: even government agencies change locations or telephone numbers—you should periodically check to be certain of the current information.*

I. UNITED STATES GOVERNMENT

Center for Mental Health Studies of Emergencies
National Institutes of Mental Health
5600 Fishers Lane
Rockville, Maryland 20857
(301) 443-3877

Central Intelligence Agency
McLean, Virginia 22101
Press Office: (703) 484-7676

Defense Department
The Pentagon
Washington, D.C. 20350
Defense Intelligence Agency: (202) 697-7072
Public Affairs Office: (703) 697-9312

Local Diplomatic or other offices of foreign governments: check your local telephone directory or phone embassies in Washington, D.C.

Drug Enforcement Administration
1405 I Street, N.W.
Washington, D.C. 20537
(202) 633-1000

Environmental Protection Agency
401 M Street, S.W.
Washington, D.C. 20460
(202) 382-2090

Federal Aviation Administration
800 Independence Avenue, S.W.
Washington, D.C. 20591
General inquiries: (202) 267-3484
Operations Center: (202) 426-3333
Public Affairs Office: (202) 426-3883

Federal Bureau of Investigation
Pennsylvania Avenue between 9th and 10th Streets, N.W.
Washington, D.C. 20535
Local field offices: consult telephone directory.
Public Affairs Office: (202) 324-3691
Terrorism Research and Analytical Center: (202) 324-2064
Washington Command Center: (202) 324-2805

Federal Emergency Management Agency
500 C Street, S.W.
Washington, D.C. 20472
(202) 646-2500

Office of Foreign Disaster Assistance
Agency for International Development
2201 C Street, N.W.
Washington, D.C. 20520
(202) 647-8924

Overseas Private Investment Corporation
Washington, D.C. 20527
(202) 653-2900

State Department
2201 C Street, N.W.
Washington, D.C. 20520
General inquiries: (202) 647-4000
Citizens Emergency Center (available 24 hours): (202) 647-5225
Office of Counterterrorism: (202) 647-9892
Operations Center (open 24 hours): (202) 647-1512
Press Office: (202) 647-2492
Private Sector Liaison Staff (Bureau of Diplomatic Security): (202) 647-7092
Regional or Post Security Officer at U.S. diplomatic posts abroad: consult
Security Command Center
Security Command Center (open 24 hours): (202) 647-2412
Threat Assessment Division (Bureau of Diplomatic Security): (202) 647-1864
Travel Advisories: (202) 647-3723

The White House Press Office
The White House
1600 Pennsylvania Avenue, N.W.
Washington, D.C. 20500
(202) 456-2100

U.S. Geological Survey
12202 Sunrise Valley Drive
Reston, Virginia 22092
(703) 478-0752

U.S. Public Health Service
Washington, D.C. 20201
General inquiries: (202) 645-6867
Centers for Disease Control: (202) 443-2610

II. PRIVATE SOURCES

Ackerman & Palumbo Security Consultants International
3050 Biscayne Boulevard
Miami, Florida 33137
(305) 573-0977
Services: Country analysis; defensive programs; hostage negotiations.

Aircraft Crash & Rescue Training Associates
Attention: Miland R. (Miles) Young
16085 Deer Park Drive
Dumfries, Virginia 22026
(703) 680-0996
Services: Training of firefighters; analysis of aircraft crashes; aviation safety.

Terrell E. Arnold
Route 1, Box 330
Mt. Jackson, Virginia 22842
(703) 477-3353/2063
Services: Foreign policy analysis; consultation on counterterrorism and low-intensity conflict.

AVSEC, Inc.
Dulles International Airport
P.O. Box 17393
Washington, D.C. 20041
(703) 661-8564
TWX: 710-836-0649
Services: Aviation security and training.

Blackmon Mooring Steamatic Catastrophe, Inc.
1000 Forest Park Boulevard
Fort Worth, Texas 76110
(800) 433-2940 or (817) 926-5296
Services: Catastrophe restoration services for fire, smoke, odor, and water damage.

Robert A. Blum, M.D.
1301 20th Street, N.W., Suite 204
Washington, D.C. 20036
(202) 293-2625
Services: Psychiatric consultant on counterterrorism and crisis management; victimology; hostage negotiation.

Frank A. Bolz Associates, Inc.
P.O. Box 2678
Huntington Station, NY 11746
(516) 462-9706/7
Services: Training; hostage negotiation; tactical operations.

Business Risks International
Risks International Division
Attention: Eugene Mastrangelo
1600 Wilson Blvd., Suite 704
Arlington, Virginia 22209
(703) 525-6111
Services: Information on terrorist attacks worldwide; publication of newsletters; country/regional assessments; training; consultation.

Canadian Internal Security Company
275 Slater Street, Suite 1402
Ottawa, Ontario, Canada K1P 5H9
(613) 238-2331
TELEX: 053-3320
Services: Training; security analysis.

Commercial Counterfeiting Control
14755 Ventura Boulevard, Suite 1562
Sherman Oaks, California 91403
(818) 986-8168
Services: Investigation and tracking of counterfeit products.

Control Risks, LTD
9/13 Crutched Friars
London EC3N 2JS
United Kingdom
(1) 709-0575
US Office: 4330 East-West Highway, Suite 320
Bethesda, Maryland 20814
(301) 654-2075
Services: Executive training; security analysis; preventive programs; country analysis; hostage negotiations.

Corporate Response Group
Attention: Robert Wilkerson
1818 N Street, Suite 325
Washington, D.C. 20036
(202) 775-0177
Services: Worldwide crisis management services; crisis communications.

Robert T. Dove
4663 Cahuenga Boulevard
North Hollywood, California 91602
(818) 763-3573
Services: Retired captain, Los Angeles City Fire Department; specialist in investigations and countermeasures for fires due to arson, riots, sabotage, etc.; expert witness services; bomb threat procedures.

Mary Dale Ellis
2123 California Street, N.W.
Washington, D.C. 20008
(202) 234-3571
Services: Consultation on counterterrorism and crisis management; victimology; hostage negotiation; criminology.

Essex Corporation
333 North Fairfax Street
Alexandria, Virginia 22314
(703) 548-4500
Services: Security-related operations and analysis; surveys.

Events Analysis, Inc.
12101 Toreador Lane
Oakton, Virginia 22124
(703) 620-3648
Services: Accident investigation; system safety planning and analysis; safety and health program development; safety audits; emergency response planning and evaluation; training; regulatory analysis; safety research.

The Fairfax Group, Ltd.
7369 McWhorter Place, Suite 420
Annandale, Virginia 22003
(703) 750-1070
Services: Risk and threat analysis; crisis management; contingency planning; litigation; other counterterrorist services.

Frost and Sullivan
106 Fulton Street
New York, New York 10038
(212) 233-1080
Services: Political risk assessments and forecasts.

Dr. Raymond H. Hamden
P.O. Box 230
Arlington, Virginia 22210
(202) 659-5552
Services: Consultation on psychological aspects of terrorism, hostage situations, and Islamic fundamentalism; treatment of victims of war and acts of terrorism; conflict resolution and management; political psychology.

Highflite Associates, Ltd.
Attention: Frank Johns
8420 Blakiston Lane
Alexandria, Virginia 22308
(703) 437-7251
Services: Security training; surveys; analyses.

Interests, Ltd.
6917 Arlington Road, Suite 303
Bethesda, Maryland 20814
(301) 656-6610
Services: Publication of *Counterterrorist* newsletter.

JAE Ltd.
P.O. Box 1516
Rockville, Maryland 20850
(301) 294-3120
Services: Consultation on crisis management and emergency preparedness matters.

Kanan, Corbin, Schupak & Aronow, Inc.
Attn: Dr. David Raddock
820 Second Avenue
New York, New York 10017-4504
(212) 682-6300
Services: Public relations; political risk assessment.

Richard W. Kobetz & Associates, Ltd.
North Mountain Pines Training Center
Route Two, Box 342
Winchester, Virginia 22601
(703) 955-1128 (24-hour desk)
Services: Training in many facets of security.

Robert Kupperman Associates
2832 Ellicott Street, N.W.
Washington, D.C. 20016
Attention: Robert Kupperman
(202) 775-3229
Services: Consultation on crisis management and corporate and governmental policies for coping with terrorism.

Neil C. Livingstone
610 Watergate South
700 New Hampshire Avenue, N.W.
Washington, D.C. 20037
(202) 342-0309
Services: Counterterrorism and low-intensity conflict consultation.

Louis R. Mizell
5401 Westbard Avenue, Suite 1008
Bethesda, Maryland 20816
(301) 986-9205
Services: Training; counterterrorism tactics; general security consulting.

New Dimensions International
Attention: Fred J. Villella
P.O. Box 897
Cardiff By The Sea, California, 92007
(619) 436-1241
Services: Training in numerous planning and security areas; publication of training manuals, consultation on various security-related matters.

Mayer Nudell
Specialized Consulting Services
400 Timber Lane
Falls Church, Virginia 22046-3824
Cable: CRISISMGMT   Falls Church, VA
(703) 237-2513
Services: Counterterrorism policy and response; contingency planning; crisis management; victimology; country studies; general foreign policy/national security matters; training.

Public Safety Group
Attention: Jack McGeorge
14338 Jefferson Davis Highway
Woodbridge, Virginia 22191
(703) 491-5236
Services: Explosives training and disposal; general security surveys; training.

Rand Corporation
Attention: Brian Jenkins
Santa Monica, California 90406
(213) 393-0411
Services: Research and information on various facets of terrorist activities.

Sahlen & Associates
Attention: Elmer Snow
6001 Montrose Road, Suite 508
Rockville, Maryland 20852
(301) 231-0722
Services: Executive protection; general security training.

Scotti School of Defensive Driving
Attention: Tony Scotti
10 High Street, Suite 13
Medford, Massachusetts 02155
(617) 395-9156
TELEX: 955439
Services: Driving courses; transportation security; armored vehicles; publishes newsletter.

Dr. Stephen Sloan
Department of Political Science
University of Oklahoma
Norman, Oklahoma 73019
(405) 325-6421
Services: Consultation on counterterrorism policy and operations; training;
simulations.

USATREX International, Inc.
Attention: Arthur Kim
6723 Whittier Avenue, Suite 103
McLean, Virginia 22101
(703) 448-0178
Services: Security consulting; surveys; training.

UXB International Inc.
1275 K Street, N.W., Suite 1203
Washington, D.C. 20005
(202) 898-0115
TELEX: 64473
Services: Explosives training and disposal.

Vance International
10467 White Granite Drive, Suite 210
Oakton, Virginia 22124
(703) 385-6754
Services: Guard forces; security surveys; country assessments; explosives.

Varicon International
One Skyline Place, Suite 212
5205 Leesburg Pike
Falls Church, Virginia 22041-4118
(703) 284-7890
Services: Executive protection; contingency planning; training.

Claude Watkins
11318 Fairway Court
Reston, Virginia 22090
(703) 437-3939
Services: Training in hostage survival and victimology.

WSM Publishing Company
Box 466
Merrifield, Virginia 22116
(301) 564-8473 (answering service)
TELEX: 197652 T REP WASHDC ATTN WSM PUB
Services: Publication of World Status Map (containing travel advisories and health warnings); sale of various publications dealing with international travel, terrorism, etc.

III. ASSOCIATIONS/INSTITUTES

American Foreign Service Association
2101 E Street, N.W.
Washington, D.C. 20520
(202) 338-4045
Services: Professional association of the career Foreign Service and others interested in foreign affairs; maintains information on specialists in various facets of foreign affairs.

American Red Cross
17th and D Streets, N.W.
Washington, D.C. 20036
(202) 737-8300
Services: Disaster relief; first-aid training; blood bank; miscellaneous health and medical services.

American Society for Industrial Security
1655 North Fort Myer Drive
Arlington, Virginia 22209
(703) 522-5800
Services: Association of security professionals; training; publication of *Security Management* and other materials.

Association of Contingency Planners
P.O. Box 73-149
Long Beach, California 90801-0073
Services: Exchange of experience and information among professionals interested in business recovery planning.

Association of Political Risk Analysts
113 Fifteenth Street, N.W., Suite 620
Washington, D.C. 20006
(202) 293-5913
TELEX: 292046 IMGUR
Services: Up-to-date information on worldwide trends and events; briefings on monitoring, analyzing, and managing business risks; networking among professionals involved in business risk analysis and business political intelligence gathering.

Association of State Floodplain Managers
P.O. Box 2051
Madison, Wisconsin 53701-2051
Services: Publishes newsletter; monitors federal policies associated with flood-plain management; monitors state and local floodplain management programs.

Center for Crisis Management
Attention: Dr. Ian I. Mitroff
University of Southern California
300 Bridge Hall
Los Angeles, California 90089-1421
(213) 743-8318
Services: Variety of crisis management-related services, including planning, training, and crisis communications.

Center for Disaster Studies
James Cook University of North Queensland
Townsville, Queensland
4811 Australia
Services: Publishes summaries of major disasters and conference proceedings.

Center for Technology, Environment and Development
Clark University
950 Main Street
Worcester, Massachusetts 01610
(617) 793-7711
Services: Studies issues of risk management, especially those dealing with technological hazards; maintains specialized library.

Chemical Referral Center
Chemical Manufacturers Association, Inc.
2501 M Street, N.W.
Washington, D.C. 20036
(800) 262-8200
(202) 887-1315
Services: Provides referrals to more than four hundred companies for answers to nonemergency chemical questions.

Disaster Research Center
University of Delaware
Newark, Delaware 19716
(302) 451-6618
Services: Research into sociological aspects of disasters; maintains library.

Disaster Study Group
Uppsala University
Box 513, S-75120
Uppsala, Sweden
Services: Publication of studies on sociological and psychological aspects of emergencies.

Foundation for International Human Relations
Post Office Drawer 230
Arlington, Virginia 22210-0230
(202) 387-0246
TELEX: 4996729 HUMAN
Services: Consultation on political psychology, international health care development and training, conflict resolution, and human resources management; publications.

Institute for Victims of Terrorism
6801 Market Square Drive
McLean, Virginia 22101
(703) 847-8456
Services: International network of referrals for those in need of help as a result of acts of terrorism; information and guidance on victim compensation; counseling on issues of media intrusion and other stresses; advisory and consulting services.

Institute on Terrorism and Subnational Conflict
Box 25368 Georgetown Station
Washington, D.C. 20007
(202) 429-4913
Services: Research and consultation on all facets of terrorism and other forms of low-level political violence.

International Anticounterfeiting Coalition
101 California Street
San Francisco, California 94111-5874
(415) 986-2380
TELEX: 278638
Services: Coordination of government and industry anticounterfeiting efforts; publication of newsletter.

International Association of Chiefs of Police
P.O. Box 6010
Thirteen Firstfield Road
Gaithersburg, Maryland 20878
(301) 948-0922
Services: Association of law enforcement professionals; publication of *Police Chief, Clandestine Tactics and Technology,* and other materials; training; research into law enforcement issues.

International Counterterrorism & Security Association
110 S. Weber, Suite 102
Colorado Springs, Colorado 80903
(719) 389-1258
Services: Clearing house for information, activities, and networking among professionals engaged in all aspects of counterterrorism and security.

International Disaster Institute
85 Marylebone High Street
London W1M 3DE
United Kingdom
Services: Publishes journal; clearinghouse for information on international aspects of disasters and disaster relief, especially with regard to developing nations.

International Fire Service Training Association
Fire Protection Publications
Oklahoma State University
Stillwater, Oklahoma 74078
(405) 624-5723
Services: Publication of various manuals.

National Academy of Sciences
2101 Constitution Avenue, N.W.
Washington, D.C. 20418
(202) 334-2000
Services: Publication of reports on various disaster-related issues.

National Coordinating Council on Emergency Management
7297 Lee Highway, Suite N
Falls Church, Virginia 22042
(703) 533-0251
Services: Association of professionals involved in emergency management and civil defense; publishes newsletter; training.

National Fire Protection Association
Batterymarch Park
Quincy, Massachusetts 02269
(800) 344-3555
Services: Information on fire prevention and related topics; publication of various manuals.

Risk and Insurance Management Society
205 East 42nd Street
New York, New York 10017
(212) 286-9292
TELEX: 968289
Services: Association of companies interested in risk management; publication of *Risk Management*.

IV. INTERNATIONAL ORGANIZATIONS

Australian Overseas Disaster Response Organization
P.O. Box K425
Haymarket, NSW 2000
Australia
Services: Publication of reports on relief and recovery efforts and conference proceedings.

Central Emergency Relief Organization
Government Headquarters
Bay Street
Bridgetown, Barbardos, West Indies
(809) 436-6435
Services: Regional disaster relief and related matters in the Caribbean.

Foreign Embassies/Consulates
(consult telephone directory, publications in the bibliography, or call appropriate desk at the State Department)
Services: Information on individual countries.

International Red Cross
Geneva, Switzerland
(contact via American Red Cross)
Services: See American Red Cross

United Nations Disaster Relief Coordinator
Palais des Nations
1211 Geneva 10
Switzerland
Services: UN coordinating office for disaster relief operations; publishes bi-monthly magazine.

World Health Organization/Pan American Health Organization
525 23rd Street, N.W.
Washington, D.C. 20520
(202) 861-3200
Services: Information concerning international health matters.

World Federation for Mental Health
1021 Prince Street
Alexandria, Virginia 22314
(703) 684-7722
Services: International nongovernmental coalition of individuals, professionals, and voluntary associations; mental health consultant status with United Nations; promotion of mental health collaboration across national boundaries.

THE LEGALITY OF RANSOM PAYMENTS AROUND THE WORLD

APPENDIX C

Much has been written about hostage and kidnapping incidents overseas—the no-ransom versus ransom philosophies, the tactics of negotiation, the organization of rescue attempts. What often has been overlooked is an important factor for businesses operating overseas, one that can influence their relations with governments for years after an incident: payment of a ransom and its legality.

Almost all countries have laws that prohibit the kidnapping of persons or the taking of hostages. However, most countries have not addressed the question of the ransom payment. What does this mean for those organizations or individuals who decide to pay a ransom to secure the release of a relative or corporate executive? What exposure to legal sanctions does such a payment entail—both for the organization and individual executives making such a decision and for anyone who may assist in the ransom payment?

To gain a better understanding of this potential problem for businesses operating internationally, coauthor Mayer Nudell conducted an informal survey in 1984 of some 142 nations to determine whether any laws existed that made the actual payment of a ransom illegal and how rigidly were such laws enforced. Of those countries in which such information was available, only ten had any legislation that could be applied to publish private ransom payments. When it came to the consistency and/or severity of enforcement, no definitive findings were possible. Either information was lacking or the government's record of enforcement was mixed and highly dependent on individual circumstances.

This survey found that the following countries had laws that either expressly forbid paying ransoms or could be used to sanction those who make such payments: Chile, Colombia, Cyprus, Ghana, Guatemala, Italy, Qatar, Singapore, Trinidad and Tobago, and Yugoslavia. It must be emphasized that these countries *appeared* to have such laws or capabilities and that the question of enforcement is open-ended.

While this information is limited and subject to change, organizations and individuals should take into account this additional factor in preparing contingency plans and in making decisions during incidents. Not only can the ransom decision be complicated in principle, in practice it can have previously unsuspected aftereffects that might remain with a company in a particular country and affect its operations indefinitely.

APPENDIX D

Many readers will be interested in further information about the preparation and conduct of simulations. In keeping with the overall approach of this book, we have prepared a more detailed overview of the process. *Please remember, however, the following information is a starting point for your use.* It will provide you with a suggested approach and will identify the constituent parts of that approach. Other approaches are possible and equally valid. Whichever you decide to use, you will have to address the following points if your simulation is to achieve your goal of ensuring that your organization and its personnel are prepared in case of emergency. What we are doing here is simply walking you through the steps described in chapter 9 and providing more details to help you accomplish your objectives.

STEP 1: SELECT YOUR CONTROLLERS

As we noted in chapter 9, the control team selection is extremely important. They will design the simulation, conduct it, and provide initial feedback to your personnel on the results. The size of the control team will be governed by the dimensions of your projected simulation and the number of people who will participate. There must be a sufficient number of controllers to ensure that your Crisis Action Team does not "outplay" the control team, invalidating the results of the exercise by overwhelming them. Chapter 9 identifies the minimum requirements in this regard, including our view that at least one controller *must* come from the ranks of the organization. Beyond this, factors such as physical constraints and security requirements will influence your decision.

It is important that the controllers from within your organization are protected from later victimization at the hands of players. It is the controller's job to create situations that test the organization's reactions, along with those of its personnel. If either are found lacking in any fashion, the controller is not to blame. Just as the players should not suffer in case of error (especially if it is an organizational error), neither should the controllers.

STEP 2: DETERMINE THE EXTENT OF THE SIMULATION

This is critical to the success of your simulation. Determine early the scope of the simulation. Do you wish to test all elements of an extensive emergency plan or do you wish to limit the exercise to a specific component? For example, the Department of State's Crisis Management Exercise Program endeavors to test many different parts of each embassy's Emergency Action Plan (a comprehensive plan containing sections covering all the operations that might be required in any type of emergency). This requires an extensive scenario. On the other hand, your organization may have compartmentalized its emergency planning into discrete or functional plans complete unto themselves and you may wish to test only one of them, or even only part of one of them.

Once you have determined the dimensions of your simulation, the control team should begin its efforts by reading the plan(s). In addition, if you have selected controllers from outside your organization (something we encourage for the independent perspective they can provide), you must furnish information concerning your organization, its operating procedures, and organizational culture for them to review. The more the controllers know about your organization and its personnel, the greater precision they can incorporate into the simulation.

The next item is the identification of your goals for the exercise. If you already know your requirements, you must ensure that the controllers fully understand them. If the control team is to assist you in establishing these parameters, then they should do so before tackling the details of creating the exercise.

At this point, a decision must be made on two specific operational considerations. First, you must decide if the exercise is to be conducted in real time or in compressed time. There are arguments for either choice. Real-time exercises allow events to proceed at their normal pace and expose personnel to many of the same stresses and considerations they will face in a prolonged emergency. Compressed-time exercises allow you to accomplish your objectives in a reduced time frame, shortening the time your players must devote to the exercise and magnifying the pressures under which they will work. It is important to remember that compressed time makes things happen during the exercise much faster than they do in real life, which poses problems for the controllers as well as for the players. Making this decision enables the control team to structure the exercise appropriately—including such details as scheduling breaks in the play if it is not to be a twenty-four-hour continuous operation.

Second, you must decide the extent to which you will allow free play during the exercise. Some exercises allow maximum free play by the players, which encourages the exploration of alternative strategies and tactics. Others are as completely determined (pre-scripted) as possible to provide training in already existing organizational procedures and policies. Each is appropriate for particular goals. However, considerably more work must be done where "textbook" solutions exist and all moves and responses must be worked out in advance. Your choice will relate to your goals for the exercise.

The control team now can identify the key events that must occur for the exercise to accomplish your goals. The military has developed a name for these: Major Scenario Event List, or MSELs (pronounced "measles"), for these. These will drive the exercise and must occur regardless of other considerations. They should be listed and placed in an order that can be used to guide the development of other implementors.

Now, the control team can research the props they will employ: the communications and other equipment the organization uses to respond to the type(s) of emergency and incorporated into the plan(s) being tested. This point must be stressed: *if some piece of equipment is not currently available to the organization, it should not be allowed in the exercise.* If a piece of equipment is available, then its absence in the plan should not necessarily prohibit its use *if the Crisis Action Team notes its absence and requests it.* If an available item is not requested by the players, the controllers have ways to gently remind them of its availability (for example, in the form of an offer by the home office to send one).

STEP 3: PREPARE THE BACKGROUND

Chapter 9 discussed the importance of the background piece to the exercise. Briefly restated, the background piece sets the stage for the exercise by providing any needed transitions from actual conditions to those required by the exercise scenario and provides the context within which the exercise events will occur.

It provides the credibility that enables the players to suspend their disbelief and become totally involved in the exercise.

The contents of your background piece will depend on your particular exercise. Generally speaking, the more comprehensive the exercise, the greater the detail required in the background piece. For a multinational organization of any type, your background piece will probably require a minimum of two major sections: one dealing with international affairs and a second dealing with the affairs of the country in which the exercise events will happen. Let's look at these more closely.

International. This part of the background piece will discuss political and economic events which affect the world at large. For any number of reasons, these events will be relevant to the particular country with which you are dealing, because of factors such as oil prices, foreign assistance, commercial interest rates, tariffs, boundary disputes, and elections. Governmental and military organizations will also need to factor in geopolitical and military considerations such as activities of foreign governments, regional wars, or disputes. Businesses may place less emphasis on these sorts of events, but regional considerations may be important in a particular instance.

Domestic. Many of the same sorts of events contained in the international section will be found here as well. The purpose of this section is to provide information about exactly how world political and economic developments have affected this particular country. It also provides social and cultural information relevant to circumstances in which the exercise will occur. Labor disputes, partisan politics, human rights abuses, taxes, and economic statistics can all be included. Also in this section are particular events that set the stage for the exercise-specific developments.

STEP 4: PREPARE IMPLEMENTORS

Bearing in mind the MSELs previously identified, the next step is to prepare the other implementors required for the exercise. The controllers should remember that each implementor has a specific purpose. Some may be designed to test the players' knowledge of organizational procedures and policies. Others may address various facets of public affairs, victimology, communications capabilities, and reporting criteria. Each implementor must relate to one or more goals of the exercise and should contribute to maintaining the proper atmosphere for the exercise. Too much humor can be dysfunctional. A proper balance of seriousness and tension release is essential.

It is useful from the controllers' point of view to organize the implementors into categories. This enables the construction of an organized data base that will be helpful in creating future exercises and will facilitate updating, changes, and other administrative needs, especially if the data base is computerized. It will also assist you in organizing the exercise itself.

As the implementors are developed, the controllers must keep in mind the degree of pre-scripting versus free play contained in the exercise. Especially in the case of an exercise designed to incorporate a large scope for free play, the implementors must be flexible enough to be adapted easily should the players develop an unexpected alternative tactic. In some cases, implementors will need to be eliminated completely because actions taken by the players will have rendered them moot before their scheduled use. In other cases, spare implementors will need to be used when alternative strategies can be foreseen by the controllers before the exercise.

One of the key implementors that should be incorporated into the MSEL is the concluding one. This implementor is intended to provide the Crisis Action Team with the impetus to engage in a limited amount of self-criticism and review. It may take the form of a request from headquarters for an after-action or similar report, or it could be injected as a news report or a telephone call from the local government. As long as it accomplishes its purpose, its form is optional.

The form of an implementor is simple. It should have a short title and a space for a number, which will be added after the sequence of the exercise is determined (see next section). It should also have a number related to the data base you are building (implementor number). It must identify who is doing what and with or to whom. It must also describe the method of use of the implementor (i.e., a telephone call or a telegram). Then, the proper instructions to the controller must appear. If the controller is to play a role, then he or she must know what that role is and what tone to employ. (This is one of the reasons we stress the inclusion in the control team of field or other knowledgeable personnel from the organization. This person is an invaluable asset in terms of interpersonal relationships among the players and between the players and the outside world.) The implementor sheet must also remind the controller what to look for and how to respond, if appropriate. For example, in some cases it will be necessary to have two versions of the implementor—a sanitized one for the players and a complete one for the controllers. Figure D–1 gives an example of a complete implementor. It is important that each implementor be in the proper format employed by the organization and that any appropriate procedures for particular categories of implementors (cable routings, approvals) be followed.

STEP 5: ESTABLISH ORDER AND TIMETABLE

Once the control team has developed a package of implementors, it must organize them to ensure timely injection into the exercise. An effective way to do

---

EXERCISE NO. _____   IMPLEMENTOR NO. __PR-5__

<u>MEDIA REPORTS TRANSGLOBAL SPOKESMAN DENIES RESPONSIBILITY</u>

NEWS REPORT

FROM: WIRE SERVICE (ASSOCIATED PRESS)

TO: PUBLIC AFFAIRS OFFICER

(NEW YORK, OCTOBER 25)   A spokesman at the international headquarters of Transglobal Enterprises today denied his firm's responsibility for the industrial accident in Freedonia which claimed fourteen lives and sent fifty-five people to the hospital with respiratory difficulties. He charged that Freedonia was seeking to place the blame for the accident on Transglobal instead of admitting that the government's policy of permitting public housing to be established in the immediate vicinity of Transglobal's plant was ill-conceived.

CONTROLLERS NOTE: THIS IS TO BE USED ONLY IN THE EVENT THAT THE NEW YORK AND FREEDONIAN OFFICES ARE NOT COORDINATING PUBLIC STATEMENTS. NOTE HOW LONG IT TAKES FOR THE FREEDONIAN PUBLIC AFFAIRS OFFICER TO CONTACT NEW YORK.

Figure D–1. Sample Exercise Implementor

this is to create an exercise book for each member of the control team, in which each implementor appears in the proper order. This book should be broken into convenient sections according to the exercise's timing and should begin with a clock (especially in the case of compressed timing) and a listing of the sequence in which implementors are to be used. The book should also contain a copy of the background piece, along with any documents or other introductory items given to the players.

STEP 6: TEST THE EQUIPMENT

Regardless of the size of your organization or the extent of its operations, there will be some equipment that you will rely on during emergency situations. It may be as simple as a telephone and a typewriter or as elaborate as state-of-the-art communications. Whatever it is, the exercise must incorporate its use, either directly or through simulation. It is important for the control team to establish exactly what equipment will be used and the method of simulating it.

This can be accomplished by using the equipment itself, as when organizational tielines, telephones, or telexes are employed, using a code that establishes the message as an exercise-only item, or through the creative use of closed circuit telephones or intercoms to simulate the equipment. For example, a series of telephones connected by a closed loop can be used to simulate the use of ordinary and secure telephones, and intercoms can be used to simulate radio communications. The implementors can be structured to simulate actual telex or telegraphic traffic without the necessity of employing the actual equipment.

Whatever approach you select, the controllers must ensure that *only* the equipment *actually* in place or available to the players is used during the exercise. All equipment to be employed during the exercise must be thoroughly tested before STARTEX to ensure that it is functioning properly and correctly labeled as to its identity. The controllers are responsible for this testing, with appropriate technicians. Testing should occur at the exercise site regardless of how many times the equipment has been previously tested.

STEP 7: TAILOR THE SCENARIO AND IMPLEMENTORS

Now it is time for the control team to tour areas relevant to the exercise, if it has not done so previously. This will ensure that important details such as street names and landmarks are correct and will provide information for implementors that might only be available locally. Again, the contributions of the field or local member of the controller team will be important, as the team inevitably will find that certain relationships or other details are unexpected. This is especially true when a foreign part of a multinational organization is being exercised. It is amazing just how many cultural, social, or other fine points that are materially relevant cannot be anticipated.

Part of the control team's activities at this point will include a physical survey of relevant facilities and local resources. This will assist them in verifying the resources available to the players. It will also help them learn identities of important support characters (drivers, secretaries, family members) for the players—all of which will lend the necessary authenticity.

STEP 8: THE PRE-BRIEFING

Before the exercise, the control team should meet with the players and any senior managers who will not be involved in the exercise to discuss rules and procedures. At this time the background piece and any other preexercise documents can be given to the players. An effective way to do this is to create player books that contain the background piece, the exercise clock, and the additional documents. It may also be helpful to include a brief summary of the rules and procedures, which the control team will present orally at the briefing.

In the briefing itself, the chief controller should introduce himself or herself and the entire control team. Then he or she should explain that the exercise is to be a training effort and an opportunity to evaluate the effectiveness of procedures and plans. Stressing that there will be no grades, the chief controller should outline the procedures to be followed during the exercise. Among the essential points to be covered are: with the exception of the players and their staff, the control team is the only link to the outside world; only currently existing equipment and personnel may be used or requested; if a piece of equipment or a person is deployed away from the players' location, then that equipment/person must physically be removed from the room; and that players must actually write reports, prepare messages, and, in general, accomplish the required tasks—they cannot simply tell the control team that something is to be done. (Chapter 9 discusses these points.) There will be enough artificialities in any exercise without employing counterproductive shortcuts.

Above all, the chief controller must emphasize that the control team is not there to dictate events or responses. Rather, the purpose of the exercise is to permit the Crisis Action Team and senior management to form their own conclusions about the adequacy of their plans, procedures, and expertise.

STEP 9: THE EXERCISE

As chapter 9 points out, the control team will need to ensure that the exercise remains on schedule and accomplishes its objectives. To do so, it will be necessary for at least one controller to be present at all times in the players' room. Another controller will be responsible for ensuring that implementors are injected on schedule and that a log is maintained. Other controllers will be responsible for playing designated roles and following the directions of the senior controller, who will orchestrate the exercise.

It is essential that the controllers remain in regular contact with one another through frequent, although fleeting, meetings. During these meetings, they can monitor the pace of developments and see that the rules of the exercise are being followed. They will also be able to determine if any changes are required to implementors or if any administrative time-outs (a device which essentially stops the exercise for a few minutes to enable the controllers to address any confusions among the players regarding exercise constraints) are needed.

This contact will be facilitated if the control team gives some thought to its own seating arrangements. (The player team will seat itself either according to a planned arrangement or randomly; this can be one of the areas tested.) A glance back to figure 6–1 will remind readers that the same type of configuration used in a simple ad hoc crisis management center are also applicable for controller use during an exercise.

The final part of the exercise play is the short self-critique by the players. This is not an evaluation of how realistic or effective the exercise was (that is saved for the next step), but an opportunity to begin the critical review process of the planning and execution by the organization itself.

STEP 10: THE POSTEXERCISE DEBRIEFING

The final step in the exericse process is the after-exercise meeting between the control team and the players.

Remember that this is a no-risk exercise. Therefore, this meeting should be informal and there should be no record kept of it. Any reports made should be nonspecific in terms of personnel and merely highlight general conclusions. Otherwise, the process will not work properly. This meeting should be held the day after the exercise and it will concentrate on two principal matters. First, the players will have an opportunity to question the control team on any exercise matters and to discuss the rationale behind particular actions. Second, the controllers will have an opportunity to explain again the objectives of the exercise and to provide in a general way their conclusions regarding the players' actions and the plan's procedures. Ideally, this will lead to an informal give-and-take in which the expertise of the control team can be shared with the players, without denigrating the players' efforts. Alternative actions and options can be suggested and discussed.

We cannot emphasize enough how important a good post-exercise debriefing is. We have seen excellent exercises—well-planned, well-equipped, and well-executed—thoroughly ruined by a poor debriefing. One of the quickest routes to a dead end is a control team that doesn't know when to stop talking.

At the end of a successful exercise, most of the players will be "up." They will have many questions, be eager for feedback and suggestions, and want to talk over their experiences. A control team, or team member, who insists on turning the meeting into a classroom lecture will squelch that enthusiasm and undercut most of the pedagogic value of the exercise. The controllers must *let the players talk*. They should guide the discussion, offer suggestions, and be as supportive as possible. But the value of a simulation is in the ideas of the players.

Similarly, there may be questions and disagreements about specific points in the exercise. Controllers should be able to clarify and justify these points, but they should keep an open mind. The questioning done by the players is part of the learning process also. Sometimes even the controllers can learn something.

An important responsibility of the control team at this meeting is to provide a transition from the exercise environment back to normal working conditions. This is especially important if there were any clashes (personality or otherwise) among the players during the exercise. If the control team can provide the proper bridge, players will be able to place the events of the exercise in context and resume their professional relationships. Controllers and organizations should recognize, however, that there is always the possibility that a particular player may prove unsuited to emergency action responsibilities, or that the results of the exercise dictate permanent changes.

CONCLUSION

Simulations are not a short cut to emergency planning. They do, however, allow you to test and refine the fruits of your labors. In this way, your organization can experiment with new approaches to recurring problems or attempt to confront new challenges to its operations. Whatever the case, no emergency planning program can be considered complete without this important tool.

NOTES

CHAPTER 1

1. As used by the Office of Foreign Disaster Assistance of the U.S. Agency for International Development and the Pan American Health Organization.
2. Extracted from the June 1987 edition of *Disaster History*, published by the Office of Foreign Disaster Assistance, U.S. Agency for International Development.
3. *Ibid*.
4. According to "Ripley's Believe It or Not," *Washington Post*, June 28, 1987.
5. According to Stephen A. Thompson of the Department of Geography at the University of Colorado, *Geo* magazine, December 1982, p. 117.
6. According to James Cornell, *The Great International Disaster Book*, pp. 6–7.

CHAPTER 2

1. As defined in the unabridged edition of *The Random House Dictionary of the English Language*.
2. For a thorough discussion of the precrisis, or "prodromal" stage of crisis management, see Steven Fink's *Crisis Management: Planning for the Inevitable*.
3. According to the Pan American Health Organization.

4. This definition will be sufficient for our purposes, given that this handbook is intended to help readers plan for emergencies, regardless of what they are called.

CHAPTER 3

1. See Richard I. Kirkland, Jr., "Union Carbide: Coping with Catastrophe," *Fortune*, 7 January 1985, p. 52.

CHAPTER 4

1. Excerpted from press reports.
2. Beatrice Foods was sued by one of its employees who had been the victim of a kidnapping, despite the corporation's successful negotiation of his release via a ransom payment. Exxon was once sued by stockholders who objected to the size of a ransom payment.
3. For a general discussion of the importance of advance consideration of crisis preparations, see Mayer Nudell "Contingency Planning: A Must for Business" in vol. X, issue X of *Clandestine Tactics and Technology*, a publication of the International Association of Chiefs of Police.
4. See Norman Antokol and Mayer Nudell, "Generic Contingency Planning for Terrorist Incidents," vol. XI, issue 8, *Clandestine Tactics and Technology*.
5. There may even be more than twenty-two, but the following list will suffice to illustrate the potential dimensions of this problem. Our twenty-two categories are based upon a multinational organizational structure. (1) Home-country executives serving in a foreign country. (2) Home-country nonexecutive staff serving in a foreign country. (3) Home-country executives, based at headquarters, traveling abroad on official business. (4) Home-country executives, based at headquarters, traveling on unofficial business. (5) Home-country nonexecutive staff, based at headquarters, traveling abroad on official business. (6) Home-country nonexecutive staff, based at headquarters, traveling on unofficial business. (7) Board members or other advisory/consulting personnel traveling on organizational business. (8) Board members or other advisory/consulting personnel traveling on nonorganizational business. (9) Local employees, citizens of the country in which the emergency occurs. (10) Third-country national employees. (11) Local agents/sales representatives. (12) Families of home-country executives. (13) Families of executives based abroad. (14) Families of executives accompanying him or her on a business trip. (15) Families of nonexecutive home-country staff. (16) Families of executives accompanying him or her on a nonbusiness trip. (17) Families of nonexecutive staff based abroad. (18) Families of nonexecutive staff accompanying him or her on a business trip. (19) Families of nonexecutive staff accompanying him or her on a nonbusiness trip. (20) Families of local employees. (21) Families of third-country nationals. (22) Families of local agents/sales representatives.
It should be noted that local or third-country employees may or may not be at the executive level. Local employees are defined as those employees who are of the same nationality as the foreign country in which they are working, while third-country national employees are citizens of a different country than the one in which they are

working. Additionally, the very definition of who is to be included in the term "family" must be clearly understood, as the family unit varies widely throughout the world.

6. This is another truism we learned during our years in the State Department. Embassy security officers have told us repeatedly that they lacked authority to implement needed security measures, yet they—not the ambassador or anyone else—were held responsible should anything happen. This attitude has changed. The department has issued guidance to the effect that senior decision-makers are accountable for their actions or inactions.

7. This was brought home to us during a 1983 terrorist incident in Honduras. After the incident was successfully resolved, an interagency *post mortem* was held and a number of problems we had encountered were addressed only because we had kept a detailed record of activities.

CHAPTER 5

1. As one example of the input legal counsel can bring to crisis management planning, consider the fact that the Price-Anderson Act of 1957, as amended, limits a nuclear plant operator's liability for a Chernobyl-style occurrence to $700 million for a single accident. While not an insignificant sum, this amount is nowhere near the total costs. This brings up a number of considerations that governmental agencies should bear in mind, as well as the suggestion that nuclear plant operators can approach their own contingency planning in the knowledge that their liability is not open-ended. In 1986, the House passed a bill to raise the liability for such incidents to $7.4 billion, but the Senate did not act. See also, "Nuclear Power and Nuclear Clout" by Jack Anderson and Dale Van Atta, *Washington Post*, September 11, 1987, p. E5.

2. A full discussion of this aspect of crisis management appears later in this book. At this point, we would like to make a few general points. Victims and their families may or may not have had any training or preparation for dealing with the particular type of emergency now confronting them. We highly recommend that organizations offer such training to employees and families when identifiable risks are present, such as terrorist threats, political unrest, natural threats (earthquakes, hurricanes, floods.) Likewise, if there is a risk of some type of industrial accident at the organization's facility, adequate preparation for responding to it is essential.

   During an incident, victims will be under the additional stress of worrying about their families and, possibly, feeling guilty for not having "put things in order" (a very common syndrome). Pre-existing medical problems may resurface and new ones— sometimes psychosomatic—may appear. Afterward, a period of adjustment will be required, often a prolonged one.

   As this brief overview and our more comprehensive discussion later demonstrate, there will be plenty of work for a victim/family liaison.

3. In recent years, a term has been popularized to describe people who become so enmeshed in details that they interfere with the functioning of an organization and its personnel and, in so doing, create more problems than they solve. It is "micromanagement."

4. For an excellent discussion of this and other elements of crisis management, see Stephen Fink's *Crisis Management: Planning for the Inevitable.*

5. The team must be alert to the possibility of "circular reporting," reports that seem to come from different sources and that provide corroboration of the initial information,

but which, upon investigation, are found to all come from the same source via a number of different channels.

6. A look ahead to figure 9–1 in chapter 9 will provide a graphic depiction of the dynamic planning process as we conceive it—a process that includes after-event evaluations and modifications as important elements.

7. In this context, the question of accountability must be considered. There is always a tendency to search for a scapegoat to take the blame for any failures and a stampede for accolades where success has occurred. The organization should establish clear procedures to identify those responsible for key issues related to the emergency, such as: the planning process, security preparations, logistics, equipping of the Crisis Management Center, and so forth. If these people had the appropriate authority to perform their function, then they should be held accountable for how well they did their jobs. If, however, as is often the case, responsibility and authority were diffuse prior to the emergency, then it becomes difficult to point a finger at any individual. Rather, it is the failing of the most senior people in the organization for having permitted such poor organization in the first place.

8. Imagine what you would do if, as has happened to us on various occasions, you had only a very short time to provide detailed information for a congressional committee concerning events over a period of years that had occurred several years previously. Would you want to have only your memory for reference?

CHAPTER 6

1. Compiled from press reports.

2. See the authors' "Generic Contingency Planning for Terrorist Incidents," *Clandestine Tactics and Technology*, vol. XI, issue 8, p. 5.

3. Note that this configuration presupposes that, because of the relatively small size of the organization, the Crisis Action Team will be small and that many of the functions we discuss in chapter 5 will be distributed among this smaller group.

CHAPTER 7

1. For information on other examples of where untimely press coverage has complicated the resolution of a number of hostage/barricade and other terrorist situations, see Michael Ledeen's "Bums" in *The American Spectator*, September 1986, pp. 26, 30.

2. For fuller information on this study, see Nimmo, Dan and James E. Combs, *Nightly Horrors: Crisis Coverage in Television Network News*.

3. The Weather Bureau puts out hurricane watches, storm warnings, and blizzard alerts. The State Department publishes Travel Advisories and Threat Alerts. Other organizations issue specific information in the forms of: NOTAMs (Notification To All Mariners), Small Craft Warnings (from the Coast Guard), etc.

4. The Black September terrorist group had taken these and other diplomats hostage. During the negotiations, President Nixon said publicly that the United States would not negotiate with terrorists. The terrorists learned of this via radio news reports and the three diplomats were killed as a demonstration of seriousness.

5. Occasionally, a modest amount of straight news reporting can satisfy everyone. In 1983, during an incident in which five foreign missionaries were held captive by a rebel southern Sudanese force, the rebel group demanded that the Voice of America, the BBC, and various other media carry the text of a manifesto. While this was not done, various short news items about the incident were broadcast and heard by the rebels. This satisfied them and enabled us to pass the first deadline imposed.

6. One of the authors once had the unnerving experience of having a freelance stringer for a major newspaper repeat to his superior the gist of a conversation. We can't stress this point enough!

CHAPTER 8

1. The immediate victim(s), of course, would fall into our "visible" category. Family and friends would form a transitional stage between "visible" and "invisible" victims. The members of the Crisis Action Team would be among the "invisible" victims.

2. For example, the odds of a person's dying in one of the following ways are: motorcycle accident, one in five thousand; fire, one in fifty thousand; aircraft accident, one in two hundred fifty thousand, according to Don Yalung-Mathews of the National Safety Council. See "Americans Are Crazy About Sweepstakes," *Washington Post*, June 28, 1987, p. H6. Furthermore, it has been said that an American has a 1-in-276 chance of slipping and being injured in a bathtub—a seemingly greater risk than of falling victim to a terrorist or being caught up in an earthquake.

3. Among hostage negotiators, there is a bromide about the inadvisability for hostage-takers to take only one or two hostages. The story goes that, should the hostage-taker have only one hostage and decide to kill him or her, then nothing stands between the authorities and the criminal. Therefore, one hostage is worthless. Two are no better, because if anything happens to one of the hostages, then the criminal will have only one hostage, which, as we just said, is of no practical value.

4. One particularly noteworthy example is the report that the game of Chinese Checkers was developed by an Irishman imprisoned by the British during the 1920s.

5. We recall that during discussions we had in 1983 and 1984 with the FBI during preparations for the Los Angeles Olympics, we were told that this effect had been simulated during exercises and that even trained police officers and others reported similar feelings.

6. The three characteristics of the Stockholm Syndrome (not all of which are necessarily always present) are: (1) positive identification by the hostage with the captor; (2) negative feelings by the hostage toward the authorities; and (3) positive feelings by the captor toward the hostage.

7. One of the few arguments the authors ever had occurred while we were both working in the State Department's Office of Counterterrorism and Emergency Planning. During one difficult terrorist situation, one of us wanted something done immediately and offered to do it himself if the other couldn't. The offer was rejected and a short argument ensued. Five minutes later, having recognized what had happened, we both took a break to smoke a couple of cigars and patch things up.

CHAPTER 10

1. When possible, the debriefing leader should have the assistance of someone knowledgeable about the internal dynamics of the organization: corporate culture, chain of

command, operating techniques, etc. This will enable the debriefing leader to identify key areas that might otherwise go unrecognized. However, our earlier point about keeping matters confidential should not be jeopardized for the sake of such assistance.

SELECTED BIBLIOGRAPHY

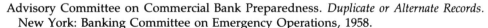

Advisory Committee on Commercial Bank Preparedness. *Duplicate or Alternate Records.* New York: Banking Committee on Emergency Operations, 1958.

———. *Continuity of Management and Alternate Headquarters.* New York: Banking Committee on Emergency Operations, 1958.

American Red Cross. *Expect the Unexpected.* Washington, D.C.: American Red Cross, 1986.

Anderson, Dale. *Developing a Crisis Management Plan for Banks.* Washington, D.C.: American Bankers Association, 1979.

Anderson, Jack, and Dale Van Atta. "Nuclear Power and Nuclear Clout." In the *Washington Post*, September 11, 1987: E5.

———. "One Third of World's Natural Disasters Occur in U.S." *Geo* magazine, (December), 117.

Antokol, Norman, and Mayer Nudell. "Generic Contingency Planning for Terrorist Incidents." In *Clandestine Tactics and Technology* XI, (8), 1986.

Asencio, Diego and Nancy. *Our Man is Inside.* Boston: Little, Brown, 1983.

Blyskal, Jeff and Marie. *PR: How the Public Relations Industry Writes the News.* New York: William Morrow, 1985.

Bolz, Frank A., Jr.. *How To Be a Hostage and Live.* Secaucus, N.J.: Lyle Stuart, 1987.

Broder, James F. *Risk Analysis and The Security Survey.* Boston, Butterworth, 1984.

Bureau of Diplomatic Security, et al. *Managing Before, During and After a Crisis.* Washington, D.C.: U.S. Department of State, 1986.

————. *Crisis Work, Crisis Worker.* Washington, D.C.: U.S. Department of State, 1986.

Carlton, Yvonne A. "The Plan's the Thing." In *Security Management* 31(8), August 1987, 71–72.

Charles, Michael T., and John Choon K. Kim. *Crisis Management: A Casebook.* Springfield, Ill.: Charles C. Thomas, 1988.

Christopher, Elizabeth M., and Larry E. Smith. *Leadership Training Through Gaming: Power, People and Problem-solving.* New York: Nichols, 1987.

Conrad, Peter. *Television: The Medium and Its Manners.* Boston: Routledge & Kegan Paul, 1982.

Cornell, James. *The Great International Disaster Book.* New York: Scribners, 1976.

Corporate Public Policy Division. *Terrorism: The Corporate Implications.* New York: Business International Corporation, 1984.

Crelinsten, Ronald D., and Denis Szabo. *Hostage-Taking.* Lexington, Mass.: Lexington Books, 1979.

Degenhardt, Henry W. *Political Dissent: An International Guide to Dissident, Extra-Parliamentary, Guerrilla and Illegal Political Movements.* Detroit: Gale Research Company, 1983.

Desowitz, Robert S. *New Guinea Tapeworms and Jewish Grandmothers: Tales of Parasites and People.* New York: W.W. Norton, 1987.

Federal Aviation Administration. *Directory: Local Law Enforcement Organizations Participating in Aviation Security.* Washington: U.S. Department of Transportation, periodic.

Federal Emergency Management Agency. *FEMA Publications Catalog.* Washington, D.C.: Federal Emergency Management Agency, periodic.

————. *Local Government Emergency Planning.* Washington D.C.: Federal Emergency Management Agency, 1982.

————. *Disaster Operations: A Handbook for Local Governments.* Washington, D.C.: Federal Emergency Management Agency, 1972.

————. *Guidance for Emergency Response Team Planning.* Washington, D.C.: Federal Emergency Management Agency, 1985.

Fink, Steven. *Crisis Management: Planning for the Inevitable.* New York: American Management Association, 1986.

Francis, Dick. *The Danger.* New York: Fawcett Crest, 1984.

Gallagher, Richard J. "Crisis Management: The Need—The Response." In *Clandestine Tactics and Technology,* 1980.

Geiger, Steven. "Developing a Workable Survivor Support Policy." In *The Police Chief* LII, (2) February 1985, pp. 56–58.

Goldberg, Andrew, et al. *Leaders and Crisis: The CSIS Crisis Simulations.* Washington, D.C.: Center for Strategic and International Studies, 1987.

Guerrier, Dennis, and Joan Richards. *State of Emergency.* Boston: Houghton Mifflin, 1970.

Hacker, Frederick J. *Crusaders, Criminals, Crazies: Terror and Terrorism in Our Time.* New York: W.W. Norton, 1976.

Hannaford, Peter. *Talking Back to the Media.* New York: Facts on File, 1986.

International Fire Service Training Association. *Field Operations Guide.* Stillwater, Okla.: Fire Protection Publications, 1983.

————. *Incident Command System.* Stillwater, Okla.: Fire Protection Publications, 1983.

Jones, Clarence. *How to Speak TV.* Marathon, Fla.: Video Consultants, 1983.

Janke, Peter. *Guerrilla and Terrorist Organizations: A World Directory and Bibliography.* Brighton, Sussex, United Kingdom: Harvester Press, 1983.

Kemp, Roger L. "The Public Official's Role in Emergency Management." In *The Police Chief* (6): June 1985, pp. 42–43.

Kentsmith, David K. "Hostages and Other Prisoners of War." In *Military Medicine* 147, November 1982, pp. 969–972.

Kobetz, Richard W., and H.H.A. Cooper. *Target Terrorism: Providing Protective Services.* Gaithersburg, Md.: International Association of Chiefs of Police, 1978, pp. 160–174.

Laur, Timothy M. *The Handbook of International Terrorism and Political Violence.* Arlington, Va.: Asian Press, 1987.

Leavitt, Harold J. *Managerial Psychology.* 2nd ed. Chicago: University of Chicago Press, 1964.

Ledeen, Michael. "Bums." In *The American Spectator*, September, 1986, pp. 29–30.

Long, Kim, and Terry Reim. *Fatal Facts.* New York: Arlington House, 1986.

Ludlum, David M. *The Weather Factor.* Boston: Houghton Mifflin, 1984.

May, Earl W. *Embassy Double Directory.* WSM Publishing Co., Box 466, Merrifield, Va., 22116.

Messick, Hank, and Burt Goldblatt. *Kidnapping: The Illustrated History.* New York: The Dial Press, 1974.

Midgley, Sarah, and Virginia Rice, eds. *Terrorism And The Media In The 1980s.* Washington, D.C.: The Media Institute, 1984.

Miller, Abraham H., ed. *Terrorism: The Media And The Law.* Dobbs Ferry, N.Y.: Transnational, 1982.

Myers, Gerald C., and John Holusha. *When It Hits the Fan: Managing the Nine Crises of Business.* Boston: Houghton Mifflin, 1986.

Nagelschmidt, Joseph S., ed. *The Public Affairs Handbook.* New York: AMACOM, 1982.

National Fire Protection Association. *Fire in Your Home.* Quincy, Mass.: National Fire Protection Association, 1978.

Nimmo, Dan, and James E. Combs. *Nightly Horrors: Crisis Coverage In Television Network News.* Knoxville: The University of Tennessee Press, 1985.

Nudell, Mayer. "Simulating Crises: The Emergency Manager's Tool." In *Clandestine Tactics and Technology* XII (7), 1987.

———. "A Blueprint for Contingency Planning." In *Security Management* 30, (5), May 1986, pp.119–121.

———. "Training for Counter-terrorism." In *Military Technology*, August 1985, pp. 20–25.

Nylen, Lars, and Örjan Hultåker. "Communication in Disaster Situations." In *The Police Chief* LIV (6), June 1987, pp. 28–34.

Office of Counterterrorism. *Patterns of Global Terrorism.* Washington, D.C.: U.S. Department of State, annually.

Office of Security. *Hostage Taking: Preparation, Avoidance, and Survival.* Washington, D.C.: U.S. Department of State, 1984.

Office of U.S. Foreign Disaster Assistance. *Disaster History: Significant Data on Major Disasters Worldwide, 1900–Present.* Washington, D.C.: U.S. Agency for International Development, June 1987.

Overseas Security Advisory Council. *Crisis Management Guidelines.* Washington, D.C.: U.S. Department of State, 1986.

Petit, Michael. *Peacekeepers at War: A Marine's Account of the Beirut Catastrophe.* Boston: Faber & Faber, 1986.

Pinsdorf, Marion K. *Communicating When Your Company Is Under Siege: Surviving Public Crisis.* Lexington, Mass.: Lexington Books, 1987.

Post, Richard S., and Arthur A. Kingsbury. *Security Administration.* 3rd ed. Springfield, Ill.: Charles C. Thomas, 1977, pp. 665–734.

Purnell, Susanna W., and Eleanor S. Wainstein. *The Problems of U.S. Businesses Operating Abroad in Terrorist Environments.* Santa Monica, Calif.: Rand, 1981.

Raddock, David M. *Assessing Corporate Political Risk.* Totowa, N.J.: Rowman & Littlefield, 1986.

Rahe, Richard H., and Glen Genender. "Adaptation to and Recovery from Captivity Stress." In *Military Medicine* 148, (7), July 1983, pp. 577–585.

Rosie, George. *The Directory of International Terrorism.* New York: Paragon House, 1987.

Schachter, Hindy Lauer. *Public Agency Communication: Theory and Practice.* Chicago: Nelson-Hall, 1983.

Sickmann, Rocky. *Iranian Hostage: A Personal Diary of 444 Days in Captivity.* Topeka, Kans.: Crawford Press, 1982.

Sloan, Stephen. *Simulating Terrorism.* Norman, Okla.: University of Oklahoma Press, 1981.

Spitzer, Cindy, "Stress: The Invisible Toll on Rescue Workers," *Washington Post*, Health Supplement, May 10, 1988, pp. 12–17.

Stratton, John G., and Barbara Tracy Stratton. "Police Widows: Dealing with Loss." In *The Police Chief* LIII (2), February 1986, pp. 40–44.

Strentz, Thomas. "The Stockholm Syndrome: Law Enforcement Policy and Ego Defenses of the Hostage." Research paper. Special Operations and Research Staff, FBI Academy. Quantico, Va, n.d.

———. "Preparing the Person with High Potential for Victimization as a Hostage." Research paper. Special Operations and Research Staff, FBI Academy. Quantico, Va, n.d.

Terrorist Research and Analytical Center. *FBI Analysis of Terrorist Incidents in the United States.* Washington, D.C.: Federal Bureau of Investigation, annually.

U.S. Department of State. *Key Officers of Foreign Service Posts: Guide for Business Representatives.* Washington, D.C.: U.S. Government Printing Office.

———. *Diplomatic List.* Washington, D.C.: U.S. Government Printing Office.

———. *Foreign Consular Officials.* Washington, D.C.: U.S. Government Printing Office.

Villella, Fred J. *Risk Assessment—Contingency Planning.* New Dimensions International, October 1986.

Western Union. "How to Develop a Crisis Communications Plan." Western Union Electronic Mail.

———. "When Every Second Counts . . . Crisis Communications Planning." Western Union Electronic Mail.

Wiend, William G., ed. "The Headquarters Fire of 1984." *Postal Inspection Service Bulletin,* Spring 1985 pp. 2–7.

Wilson, Jerry V., and Paul Q. Fuqua. *The Police & The Media.* Boston: Educational Associates, 1975.

Winston, Brian. *Misunderstanding Media.* Cambridge, Mass.: Harvard University Press, 1986.

INDEX

ABOUT THE AUTHORS

MAYER NUDELL is a former U.S. diplomat who served in El Salvador and Nicaragua during the late 1970s. He also held numerous positions at the Department of State, including two years in the Office of Counterterrorism and Emergency Planning, where he was responsible for Latin American and Middle Eastern matters and for liaison with the law enforcement, business, and intelligence communities. Now an independent consultant, he advises governmental, law enforcement, and private sector organizations on all facets of crisis management, contingency planning, and counterterrorism, and he is an instructor at the General Services Administration's Training Center. Before entering the Foreign Service, he served as an analyst for the Tunisian government's Ministry of Planning.

Mr. Nudell is a member of the American Foreign Service Association, the International Counterterrorism and Security Association, the American Society for Industrial Security (where he is chairman of the Washington chapter's Terrorist Activities Subcommittee), and the International Association of Chiefs of Police. He is also the Chairman of the Law Enforcement and Human Relations Advisory Commission of the City of Falls Church, Virginia.

NORMAN ANTOKOL, a former political science professor, is a foreign service officer. His overseas service includes tours in Caracas, London, Bridgetown, Barbados, and with the Multinational Force and Observers in the Sinai. For two years he was the public affairs officer for the State Department's Office of Counterterrorism and Emergency Planning, as well as holding the aviation, European, and African portfolios. At publication time, he was scheduled to become deputy coordinator for political training at the School of Professional Studies of the Department of State's Foreign Service Institute, the training school for the U.S. diplomatic corps. In that capacity, he will teach political tradecraft to U.S. diplomats and coordinate the teaching of ancillary subjects.

Mr. Antokol has written previously on many facets of crisis management and other national security topics for a variety of specialized and general readership publications. He has spoken on these topics to many government, private sector, and academic organizations.